TO:

_____

FROM:

Bible Stories, Devotions, & Prayers About the Names of God

I AM

40 REASONS to TRUST GOD

Diane Stortz • Illustrated by Diane Le Feyer

A Division of Thomas Nelson Publishers

I Am

© 2016 by Diane Stortz

Published in Nashville, Tennessee, by Tommy Nelson. Tommy Nelson is an imprint of Thomas Nelson. Thomas Nelson is a registered trademark of HarperCollins Christian Publishing, Inc.

Tommy Nelson titles may be purchased in bulk for educational, business, fund-raising, or sales promotional use. For information, please e-mail SpecialMarkets@ThomasNelson.com.

Unless otherwise noted, Scripture quotations are taken from the ESV® Bible (The Holy Bible, English Standard Version®). Copyright © 2001 by Crossway, a publishing ministry of Good News Publishers. Used by permission. All rights reserved.

Scripture quotations marked AMP are taken from the Amplified® Bible. Copyright © 1954, 1958, 1962, 1964, 1965, 1987 by The Lockman Foundation. Used by permission. (www.Lockman.org)

Scripture quotations marked GW are taken from *God's Word*®. Copyright © 1995 God's Word to the Nations. Used by permission of Baker Publishing Group. All rights reserved.

Scripture quotations marked ICB are taken from the International Children's Bible®. Copyright © 1986, 1988, 1999 by Thomas Nelson. Used by permission. All rights reserved.

Scripture quotations marked NLT are taken from the *Holy Bible*, New Living Translation. © 1996, 2004, 2007, 2013 by Tyndale House Foundation. Used by permission of Tyndale House Publishers, Inc., Carol Stream, Illinois 60188. All rights reserved.

ISBN-13: 978-0-529-12066-3

Library of Congress Cataloging-in-Publication Data

Stortz, Diane M., author.
  I am : 40 reasons to trust God : Bible stories, devotions, & prayers about the names of God / Diane Stortz ; illustrated by Diane Le Feyer.
    pages cm
  Audience: Ages 4 to 8.
  ISBN 978-0-529-12066-3 (hardcover)
  1. God--Name--Biblical teaching--Juvenile literature. 2. God--Juvenile literature. I. Le Feyer, Diane, illustrator. II. Title.
  BT180.N2S76 2016
  231--dc23

                              2015024140

Printed in China

17 18 19 20 LEO 6 5 4

Mfr: LEO / Heshan, China / April, 2017 / PO #9440334

For Solomon —DS

Contents

STORIES FROM THE NEW TESTAMENT

A Letter to Parents

Dear Parents,

Whenever we meet someone new, the first questions we usually ask are "What is your name?" and "What do you do?" We're interested in getting to know this new acquaintance better, and most of the time, a name alone doesn't tell us anything about this person's character or activities.

But if we want to get to know God better, learning His names is a very good place to start. That's because each of God's names in the Bible tells us something about who He is, what He is like, or what He does.

The stories in this book begin with Genesis and end with Revelation. Although the focus is on God's names, the overall story of the Bible—God's plan from before creation to someday send Jesus, the One who would make things right again—is clearly presented too.

Some of the Bible's names for God are actually descriptive titles, but for the sake of simplicity, the forty names and titles in this book are all referred to as names. With each one is a Bible story that gives young children an age-appropriate example of the meaning of the name. My prayer is that through these forty stories and the short devotions and prayers that accompany them, children everywhere will develop their understanding of God's character, learn to know Him better, and grow to love Him more.

May Psalm 9:10 be true for you and your child as you explore the names of our loving, majestic God together: "Those who know your name put their trust in you."

Diane Stortz
Making Him known to
the next generation

Stories from the
Old Testament

A Very Good World!

In the beginning, God created the heavens and the earth.
—Genesis 1:1

FROM GENESIS 1–2. Long ago, God made everything out of nothing. First, God made the world, and then He began to fill it with beauty.

God said, "Let there be light." And right away, light shone all around. God knew it was good. He parted the light from the darkness. God called the light *day*, and He called the darkness *night*. Evening came, then morning—the world was one day old.

On the second day, God said, "Let there be sky," and the sparkling blue heavens appeared. Evening came, then morning—the world was two days old.

Next God said, "Waters, gather together so dry land can appear." The waters obeyed! God called the waters *seas*, and He called the dry land *earth*. God liked what He saw—it was good!

"Now let plants and trees grow up out of the earth," God said, "each with its own kind of seed." *Pop, pop, pop!* Plants with colorful, crunchy vegetables and sweet-smelling flowers sprang out of the ground. Trees grew tall and bloomed with delicious fruit. God liked what He saw—it was good! Evening came, then morning—the world was three days old.

On the fourth day, God decorated the sky. "Let there be lights in the heavens," He said. God made the sun for the day and the moon for the night. And He made the stars—so many stars that only He could count them all! God knew it was good. Evening came, then morning—the world was four days old.

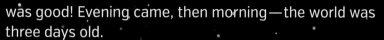

We live in a colorful, wonderful world with amazing sights and sounds. Someone powerful and loving made it all!

On the fifth day, God said, "Now for the living creatures! First let's fill the seas and the heavens. Let there be big and small creatures to swim in the seas and birds to fly through the air." *Swish! Splash! Swoosh!* Fish and turtles and whales swarmed through the seas, and birds winged their way over the earth. God liked what He saw—it was good! Evening came, then morning—the world was five days old.

On the sixth day, God said, "Let there be animals on the earth." He made every kind of animal that lives on land—from the roaring jungle lion to the wiggly,

wriggly desert lizard. And God saw that it was good. But God had saved the best for last. Now the world was ready for people!

"Let us make people in our image," God said. "They will take care of this beautiful world and all the living creatures and animals." So God made a man and a woman, Adam and Eve, and He blessed them.

Evening came, then morning—the world was six days old. Everything God had made was *very* good.

And on the seventh day, God rested.

WHAT DOES IT MEAN?

Do you like to make crafts or bake cookies? It's fun to use materials like paper and glue or ingredients like flour and eggs—and maybe even chocolate chips!—to make something new. We *create* whenever we make something new out of items we already have.

God the *Creator* made the heavens and the earth—but He made everything out of nothing! No one else could ever do that. The very first name for God in the Bible is *Elohim*, which means "the highest, no one better." Only God could create our beautiful, wonderful world!

Psalm 100:3, 5 says, "God . . . made us, and we belong to him. We are his people. . . . The Lord is good. His love continues forever" (ICB). God the Creator loves the world He made, and He loves you!

Dear God, thank You for making the world. Thank You for making me, my pets, and the people I love! You are my powerful, strong Creator! I love You, God. Amen.

LEARN MORE

- Psalm 95:6 says, "Let us worship and bow down; let us kneel before the Lord, our Maker!"
- King David wrote about the Creator and the world He made. You can find what David wrote in Psalm 8.

WHAT HAPPENED NEXT?

Adam and Eve enjoyed God, the garden, and each other. They were happy! And then one day, they made a bad choice that changed everything . . .

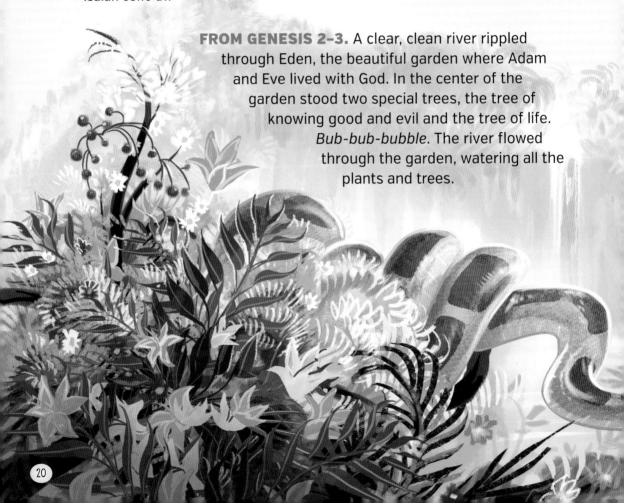

GOD OF TRUTH
El Emeth (EL *EH*-met)

A Sad Day in the Garden

Whoever asks for a blessing in the land will be blessed by the God of Truth.
—Isaiah 65:16 GW

FROM GENESIS 2–3. A clear, clean river rippled through Eden, the beautiful garden where Adam and Eve lived with God. In the center of the garden stood two special trees, the tree of knowing good and evil and the tree of life. *Bub-bub-bubble.* The river flowed through the garden, watering all the plants and trees.

God always tells the truth—He never lies. We can believe God's words!

"You may eat from every tree in the garden except the tree of knowing good and evil," God told Adam. "Do not eat from that tree, or you will die."

Now, God has an enemy who did not like Adam and Eve. One day, the enemy came to Eve disguised as a snake—a very sneaky snake. "Did God really tell you not to eat from *any* tree in the garden?" the snake asked.

"No," Eve answered. "God said we can eat from any tree except the tree in the middle of the garden. If we eat from it, we will die."

"You won't die!" the snake lied. "You'll be like God! You'll know about good and evil—that's all."

Eve listened to the snake and gazed at the fruit on the tree. *It looks so delicious!* she said to herself. *It looks so pretty! And if it can make me as wise as God* . . . Eve decided to believe what the snake told her instead of what God had said. She reached for a piece of the fruit and took a bite. She gave some to Adam, and he ate the fruit too.

Adam and Eve chewed. They swallowed. Then they looked at each other and said, "We've made a big mistake! We should have

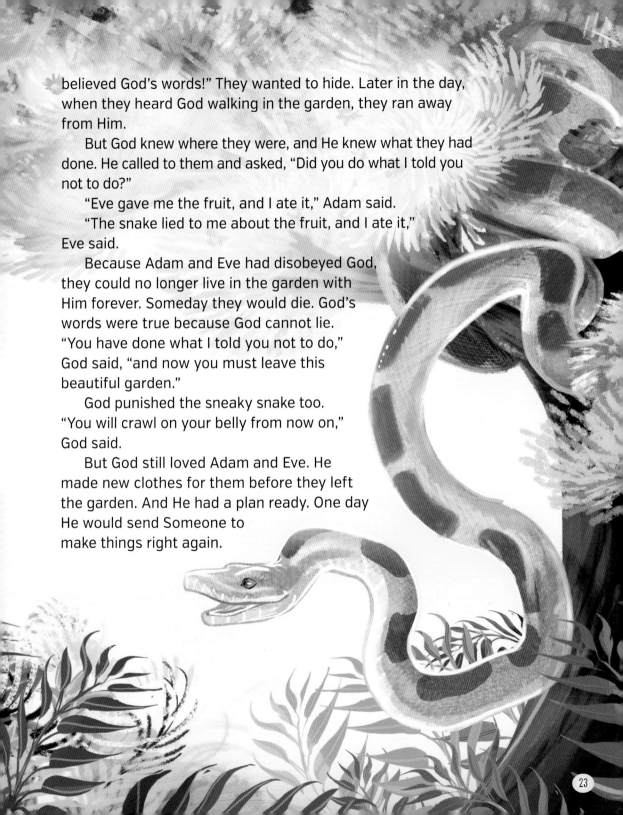

believed God's words!" They wanted to hide. Later in the day, when they heard God walking in the garden, they ran away from Him.

But God knew where they were, and He knew what they had done. He called to them and asked, "Did you do what I told you not to do?"

"Eve gave me the fruit, and I ate it," Adam said.

"The snake lied to me about the fruit, and I ate it," Eve said.

Because Adam and Eve had disobeyed God, they could no longer live in the garden with Him forever. Someday they would die. God's words were true because God cannot lie. "You have done what I told you not to do," God said, "and now you must leave this beautiful garden."

God punished the sneaky snake too. "You will crawl on your belly from now on," God said.

But God still loved Adam and Eve. He made new clothes for them before they left the garden. And He had a plan ready. One day He would send Someone to make things right again.

WHAT DOES IT MEAN?

Some games and toys use play money that doesn't look real. If you want to buy something at the store, you know you can't use a play dollar bill—you need real money! But some fake money *does* look real.

Stores need to know if money is real or fake. So cashiers practice feeling real dollar bills. They learn about small, special markings on the real dollars. When they can recognize real money, they can spot fake money too—because it is different.

One of God's names is *God of Truth*. In the Bible, God tells us what is real, or *true*—about Himself, about people, and about the world. When we know and believe God's words, which are true, then we can also recognize words that aren't true—because they are different.

What God says is always true. The God of Truth never lies. In fact, He can't! His words always prove true (Proverbs 30:5).

LEARN MORE

Hebrews 6:18 says, "It is impossible for God to lie."

WHAT HAPPENED NEXT?

People on earth disobeyed God more and more, but one man, Noah, was faithful. God saved Noah, his family, and every kind of animal from a big flood. Many years passed, until one day God spoke to another faithful man, Abraham . . .

Dear God, thank You that Your words are always true. I want to always love Your truth. Amen.

Promises for Abraham

"I am God All-Powerful. Obey me and do what is right."
—Genesis 17:1 ICB

FROM GENESIS 12–21. "Abraham," God said, "I want you to leave the town where you live and go to a land I will show you. I will bless you and make you great so all the people on earth will be blessed through you."

"Let's pack up!" Abraham told his servants and Sarah, his wife. "We need our bedrolls, tents, and cooking pots, our water jugs and lanterns. It's time for us to leave this place and go where God wants us to go."

"Yes," said Sarah, "but where *is* that?"

"God will show us," Abraham said.

And God did. God led Abraham and Sarah to the land of Canaan. "I will give this land to your family someday," God said.

"But I don't have any children," Abraham said.

"You will have a son," God said. "And you will have a *big* family. Look up at the stars. Can you count them all? No, there are too many to count. That is how big your family will be. And I will give your family all this land."

Abraham believed what God said. So he waited . . . and waited . . . and waited.

When Abraham was ninety-nine and Sarah was ninety, God spoke to Abraham again. "I am God All-Powerful," He said. "I can do anything. I will bless you and give you a big family, and I will give your family all the land of Canaan. And Sarah will have a baby boy."

God can do anything, and He keeps all His promises. Nothing is too difficult for Him!

Abraham laughed! He and Sarah were
much too old to have a baby now!

"It will happen about this time next year,"
God told Abraham.

And Abraham believed what God said. So
he waited again.

Three visitors came to see Abraham one day as he sat outside his tent under a big oak tree. Two of the visitors were angels, and one was the Lord! Abraham hurried to have a meal fixed for them, and while they ate, he stood under the tree and waited. Sarah watched and waited inside the tent.

"Sarah will have a son by this time next year," the Lord told Abraham.

This time Sarah was the one who laughed! *I'm too old to have a baby!* she said to herself.

But God is God All-Powerful, and nothing is too hard for Him. Abraham and Sarah did have a baby boy, just as God had said they would. They named him Isaac. He was the beginning of the very big family God promised to Abraham, a family that would live in the land of Canaan and bless all the people of the world.

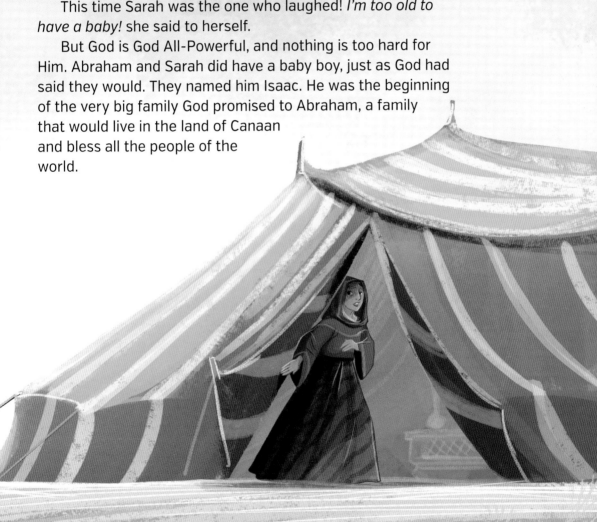

WHAT DOES IT MEAN?

Have you ever tried hard to do something, but you didn't have the power to do it? Maybe you wanted to win a race, but your legs just wouldn't go any faster and someone crossed the finish line before you. Maybe you wanted to hit a home run, but you couldn't hit the ball over the fence. Some things need power to make them happen!

Anyone can make a promise. But people don't always have the power to *keep* a promise—to do what they say they will do. Maybe your mom promised to take you swimming, but a big thunderstorm kept her from keeping her promise. Your mom doesn't have the power to stop a storm. Only *God All-Powerful* always keeps His promises—because He has the power to do it, because He is God.

God never gets tired. Psalm 121:3–4 says, "The one who watches over you . . . never slumbers or sleeps" (NLT). Nothing is too hard for Him (Genesis 18:14; Matthew 19:26). And no one else has power like God's power: "LORD, there is no one like you! For you are great, and your name is full of power" (Jeremiah 10:6 NLT).

Dear God, I feel safe because You are strong and full of power and You always keep Your promises! Thank You, God. Amen.

LEARN MORE
- Many years later, Jesus was born into Abraham's big family (Matthew 1).
- One way God kept His promise to Abraham was by sending Jesus. You can find the story of Jesus' birth in Luke 2.

WHAT HAPPENED NEXT?
Abraham and Sarah's son, Isaac, married Rebekah, and they had twin sons, Esau and Jacob. When the boys grew up, Jacob went on a long journey . . .

THE LORD IS THERE
Jehovah Shammah (jeh-HO-vuh SHAH-mah)

Jacob's Journey

The name of the city will be "The LORD Is There."
—Ezekiel 48:35 NLT

FROM GENESIS 28. *Crunch. Crunch.* Jacob looked around. Was that noise a wild animal? No, it was only Jacob's footsteps on the dry ground. Jacob didn't see any wild animals. No people either. He hadn't seen anyone else all day!

Jacob's father, Isaac, the son of Abraham, had sent Jacob on this journey. "It's time for you to get married," Isaac said. "Go visit your Uncle Laban, and marry one of his daughters."

But Uncle Laban lived so far away! Jacob had been walking all day, and he still had a long way to go. And now the sun was setting.

Jacob yawned. "This looks like a place I can sleep," he said. "And here is a big, flat stone I can use for a pillow."

Lying by himself on the ground in the dark, Jacob might have felt all alone. But God knew where Jacob was! And that night, while Jacob slept, God appeared to him in a dream.

In his dream, Jacob saw a tall ladder. The bottom of the ladder rested on the earth, and the top reached all the way to heaven. Angels went up and down the ladder, and God stood at the top and talked to Jacob.

"I am the LORD, the God of your grandfather Abraham and your father, Isaac," God said. "The promises I made to them, I am making now to you. The land where you are lying will belong to you and your family. Your family will be big—too many to be counted! And everyone in the whole world will be blessed through you and your family."

God had been with Jacob on his journey all the time, even though Jacob hadn't known it!

"I am always with you," God said. "I will take care of you everywhere you go, and someday I will bring you back to this land. I will do what I have promised."

What a wonderful dream God gave to Jacob!

When the dream ended, Jacob woke up. "God is right here with me in this place," he said, "and He has been with me all along!"

WHAT DOES IT MEAN?

Have you ever been camping? What did you do when night came and it was dark? Did you shine a flashlight all around or maybe snuggle up to your parents around a campfire? How did you feel?

All alone on his journey, Jacob might have felt lonely or afraid when he lay down to go to sleep under the stars. But he learned that God knew where he was and was right there with him.

Later in the Bible, the prophet Ezekiel wrote about a heavenly city where God will live with His people: "The name of the city will be 'The LORD Is There'" [Ezekiel 48:35 NLT]. The name of that city tells us something about God. It means God lives with us, His people. He makes His home with us—in our lives, in our families, in the church. He *wants* to be with us!

No matter where you are or how you feel, or whether it is day or night, *The LORD Is There* always knows where you are, and He is right there with you!

Dear God, wherever I am and however I feel, I know You are always with me, and that makes me glad! Amen.

LEARN MORE

When the prophet Jonah tried to run away from God, he found out God was with him everywhere—even in the belly of a big fish! You can read about it in Jonah 1–2.

WHAT HAPPENED NEXT?

Jacob married and had twelve sons, but the brothers didn't get along very well . . .

Dreams and Dreamers

Lord, my Rock, I call out to you for help.
—Psalm 28:1 ICB

FROM GENESIS 37, 39–47. "Listen to my dreams!" Joseph told his eleven brothers and his father, Jacob.

In Joseph's dreams, which came from God, eleven bundles of wheat and then eleven stars plus the sun and the moon all bowed down to Joseph. But Joseph's dreams made his brothers angry. "Do you think you're better than us?" they asked. Joseph's brothers were already upset with him. They were jealous because their father had given Joseph a beautiful, colorful coat.

One day, Jacob sent Joseph to check on his brothers, who were out in the fields, tending sheep.

"Here's our chance!" the brothers said. They grabbed Joseph, tore off his colorful coat, and threw him into a pit.

When traders with a camel caravan came by on their way to Egypt, the brothers sold Joseph to the traders. Then they went home and lied to Jacob. "A wild animal killed Joseph!" they said.

God helps us. He turns our problems into something good.

In Egypt, Joseph became a servant. He worked for Potiphar, the captain of the king's guard. God was with Joseph and made all his work turn out well. So Potiphar said, "I'm putting you in charge of everything in my house!"

Then one day, even though Joseph had done nothing wrong, Potiphar became angry with him. "Into the prison you go!" Potiphar said.

Poor Joseph! But God was still with him. The keeper of the prison put Joseph in charge of all the prisoners, and God made all Joseph's work turn out well.

Two of the prisoners, the king's baker and the king's cupbearer, had dreams they didn't understand, but God showed Joseph the meaning of their dreams. When the king's cupbearer got out of prison, Joseph said, "Please remember me."

But the cupbearer forgot all about Joseph—until two years later, when the king had strange dreams. "I know who can tell you what your dreams mean!" the cupbearer said. "His name is Joseph."

"Bring Joseph here now!" the king ordered.

The prison guards quickly brought Joseph to see the king. "Tell me your dreams," Joseph said, "and God will tell me what they mean."

Joseph listened carefully to the king, and then he said, "God is showing you what He is going to do. Seven years of good crops will be followed by seven bad years, when food will not grow. So choose someone wise who can store up grain throughout the land before the bad years come."

"You are that wise man, Joseph!" the king said. "God is with you and makes you wise. So I am putting you in charge of all the land of Egypt."

For seven good years, Joseph stored up grain. When the bad years came and people were hungry, he sold grain to them. People came from far away to buy grain. Even Joseph's brothers came! But they didn't recognize Joseph.

"Oh, my brothers!" Joseph cried. "I am Joseph! Don't be upset that you sold me into Egypt. God has helped me! He sent me here and put me in charge of all the land of Egypt so I could keep you alive! Go now and bring your families and my father here to live with me in Egypt."

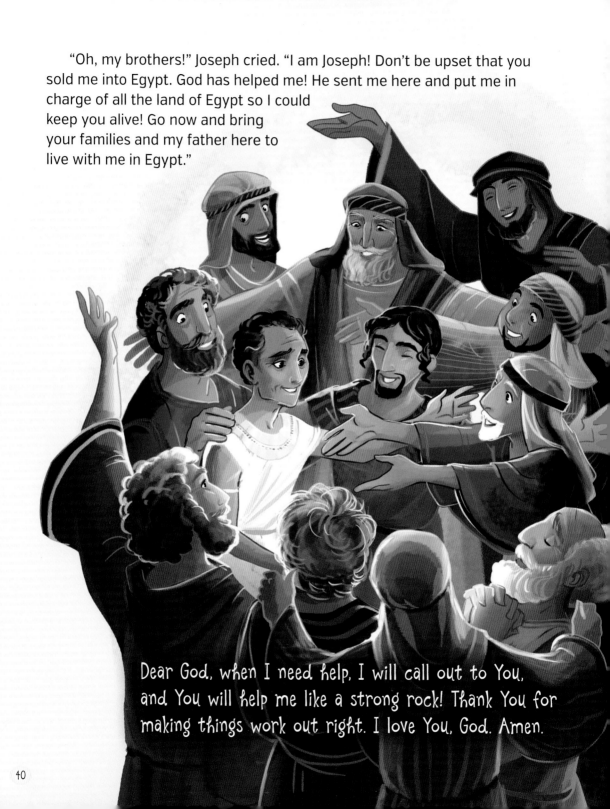

Dear God, when I need help, I will call out to You, and You will help me like a strong rock! Thank You for making things work out right. I love You, God. Amen.

WHAT DOES IT MEAN?

Have you ever climbed on playground equipment made of rope or walked across a trampoline? It's fun to try to balance on the soft surface. But when we have problems at home or at school, we want something steady to hold on to and help us!

One of God's names in the Bible is *The LORD My Rock*. Rocks are firm, strong, and solid. When we have a problem or need help, God steadies us and protects us, like a rock. We can hold on to Him. He will be with us and make things work out in a good way, just as He did for Joseph and all of Joseph's family. "There is no Rock like our God" [1 Samuel 2:2 NLT]!

LEARN MORE

- Deuteronomy 32:4 says, "He is the Rock; his deeds are perfect" (NLT).
- Jesus told a story about a man who built his house on a strong rock. Find it in Matthew 7:24–27.

WHAT HAPPENED NEXT?

Joseph's family in Egypt grew very large and became known as the Hebrews. After Joseph died, a new king in Egypt was afraid of them because there were so many, and he made them his slaves. After four hundred years of slavery, God chose a man named Moses to help His people . . .

At the Burning Bush

God said to Moses, "I AM WHO I AM. When you go to the people of Israel, tell them, 'I AM sent me to you.'"
—Exodus 3:14 ICB

FROM EXODUS 3–4. "Come, sheep!" Moses called to his flock. "It's time to move on." Moses' sheep followed him through the wilderness, *baa-baa-baaing* all the way.

As he neared Mount Sinai, Moses heard a different sound—a crackling sound, like a fire. He looked around. Yes, over there! Moses saw a bush on fire—but the bush wasn't burning up!

Moses turned toward the bush. "I want to see this amazing sight up close," he said, "and find out why the bush is not burning up."

Then Moses heard another sound, a voice calling his name. "Moses! Moses!" Who could it be?

"Here I am," Moses said.

God answered Moses from the burning bush! "Take off your sandals," God said.

"This place is holy. I am the God of your father, the God of Abraham, Isaac, and Jacob."

Moses took off his sandals and covered his face.

"I have a job for you, Moses," God said. "My people are slaves in Egypt. I know they are in trouble, and I will rescue them. I want you to lead My people out of Egypt and into a good land."

"That's a big job!" Moses said. "How can someone like me do a big job like that?"

God had no beginning, and He has no end. He never changes.

"I will be with you, Moses," God said.

Moses had another question for God. "When I tell the people that You sent me, they will want to know Your name. What should I tell them?"

"I AM WHO I AM," God said. "Tell the people that I AM has sent you. I am the God of your fathers, and this is My name forever. Now gather the leaders of My people and give them My message. Then go to the king of Egypt and tell him to let My people go."

Moses still worried about this big job. "But God, I'm not a good speaker," he said. "How can I talk to the king of Egypt?"

"I am the One who made your mouth, Moses," God said. "I will be with you and tell you what to say. I will also send your brother Aaron to help you."

Moses obeyed God. He met Aaron in the desert. Together, they went to Egypt so Moses could tell God's people, "I AM has sent me to rescue you."

"Hurrah!" the people said, and they bowed their heads and thanked God.

WHAT DOES IT MEAN?

On a cold day or a dark night, a campfire or a fire in the fireplace gives us warmth and light. (But remember—never play with matches, lighters, or fire because fire can also hurt us.) What happens to something that is on fire? It changes as it burns. When the fire goes out, only ashes are left.

But when Moses saw a burning bush, the bush was not changing. It did not burn up! That is a picture of God—He doesn't change. He always stays the same.

God never gets tired or hungry. He doesn't need anything. God always has been, and He always will be. He doesn't have a beginning or an end. He is always the same powerful God, *I AM*, who loves and helps His people.

Dear God, You never change, and You will always love and help me. Thank You, God! Amen.

LEARN MORE
- Psalm 103 praises the Lord, *Jehovah*, for His goodness.
- Jesus also used this name when He said, "Before Abraham was even born, I AM!" (John 8:58 NLT).

WHAT HAPPENED NEXT?
God began working His plan to save His people from slavery and lead them out of Egypt. He would show His mighty power to the Egyptians—who worshiped idols—too . . .

GOD WHO SAVES
El Moshaah (EL mo-shah-*AH*)

Leaving Egypt

Our God is a God who saves us.
—Psalm 68:20 ICB

FROM EXODUS 5–14. Moses and his brother, Aaron, went to see the king of Egypt, who was called Pharaoh. "God wants you to let His people, the Hebrews, leave Egypt to worship Him," they said.

"Humph!" Pharaoh said. "Why would I do that? The people are my slaves. Tell them to get back to work!" And then Pharaoh made the Hebrews' jobs even harder.

"Oh, Moses!" the people cried. "This is terrible! We are in more trouble now than we were before."

Moses asked God what to do.

"This is how to answer the people," God told Moses. "Tell them I am the Lord, and I will bring them out of Egypt. They will not be slaves any longer. I will save them with My power, and I will bring them into the land I promised to Abraham, Isaac, and Jacob."

Moses told the people what God said, but they didn't listen.

God saved His people anyway!

God began by sending troubles to the land of Egypt. The troubles were everywhere in the land—except where the Hebrews lived! First, God turned the river into blood. Then He sent frogs, then gnats, then flies. He sent sicknesses to the animals and people, hail, and locusts. He sent thick darkness to cover the land.

After each trouble ended, Pharaoh shouted, "No, no, no, the people can't go!" But then God sent one last terrible trouble, and many Egyptians died. Pharaoh changed his "No, no, no!" to "Get out! Go!"

God had already told His people to be ready to leave that night. They followed Moses and hurried out of Egypt.

Then Pharaoh changed his mind!

God rescues us when we ask Him for His help.

"I wish I hadn't let the Hebrews go," he said. "Let's chase after them and bring them all back!" In their chariots, Pharaoh and his soldiers raced to find the people.

In front of the Hebrews was a lot of water—the big Red Sea. And when the people heard Pharaoh's chariots rumbling behind them, getting closer, they were terrified. "Oh no!" they cried. "What will happen now? Who will help us?"

"Don't be afraid!" Moses said. "God will save you! Just be quiet and see how God will fight for you."

God sent a big wind. It divided the sea, making two tall walls of water. It dried up the ground at the bottom of the sea so the Hebrews could walk across on dry land!

Pharaoh's soldiers started to go across too, chasing the people. But God twisted the wheels of their chariots so they couldn't go far. When all the Hebrews had reached the other side, God sent the walls of water crashing back down into the sea on top of Pharaoh's army.

God saved His people and brought them out of Egypt, just as He said He would!

WHAT DOES IT MEAN?

When a firefighter turns on the siren of a fire truck and beeps the horn, other drivers on the road get out of the way. The fire truck and firefighters are on their way to save someone in trouble! The firefighters will do everything they can to rescue people from whatever kind of trouble they are in—whether it is a fire or some kind of an accident.

One of God's names is *God Who Saves*. God rescued, or saved, the Israelites from their hard lives of slavery in Egypt. He saved them again when Pharaoh's army chased them across the Red Sea. God saves us too! He rescues us from danger, He helps us find answers to problems, and He saves us from sin (the wrong things we do). God is the only One who can do that!

When Moses' relative Jethro heard about how God led the Hebrews out of Egypt and across the sea, he said, "Praise the Lord. He has saved all of you from the Egyptians and their king" [Exodus 18:10 ICB].

Dear God, thank You for all the ways You save me! Help me love You more every day! Amen.

LEARN MORE

When three young Jewish exiles in Babylon refused to worship a golden statue of King Nebuchadnezzar, they landed in a fiery furnace . . . but God saved them! You can read about it in Daniel 3.

WHAT HAPPENED NEXT?

The Hebrews became known as the Israelites. God led them through the wilderness toward the land He had promised Abraham. God took care of them in some amazing ways . . . .

Food from Heaven

So Abraham called the name of that place, "The Lord will provide."
—Genesis 22:14

FROM EXODUS 13, 15–16. "Follow the cloud," Moses told the people. God led the Israelites through the wilderness in a pillar of cloud during the day and a pillar of fire at night. They camped at Elim, where there was plenty of water and palm trees. Then they set out again into the wilderness.

Rumble, grumble! "I'm getting hungry, aren't you?" one person asked another.

"Yes!" "Me too!" "That's for sure!" the answers came.

The Israelites should have remembered all the ways God had already taken care of them. They should have trusted Him and asked Him to give them food to eat. But they worried and complained instead. "We wish we'd never left Egypt!" they said. "We had plenty to eat back there. Why did Moses bring us way out here anyway?"

God knows what we need and takes care of us.

God heard the people's growling tummies, and He heard their complaining too. But He still loved them, and He gave them a new way to learn to trust Him.

"Tonight I will send quail for the people to eat," God told Moses. "And in the morning I will send bread from heaven. The people will gather it every morning."

Moses and Aaron told the people, "God has heard you. Tonight you will eat meat, and in the morning you will have bread." That night, quail flew into the camp for the people to catch and eat.

The next day, early in the morning, the Israelites got up and looked outside their tents. "What are those white flakes all over the ground?" they asked in wonder.

"This is the food God promised you," Moses said. "Each of you may gather as much as you can eat today. Don't save any because God will send more tomorrow."

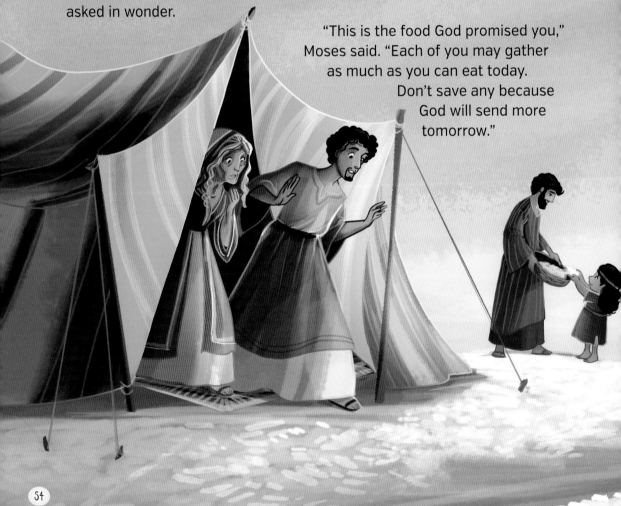

"Let's go gather it up!" the people said. "Let's try some and see how it tastes. *Mmm*, it's good, like wafers made with honey." The people called the flakes manna. They could bake bread with it or make hot cereal.

Every morning for five days, God sent new manna. Some people didn't listen to Moses though. They saved some of the manna overnight and planned to eat it the next day. But in the morning—yuck! "The manna we saved is full of worms!" the people cried. "And it smells horrible!"

Then on the sixth day, God told the people to gather enough manna for two days because the next day, the seventh day, was the Sabbath—a time for rest. There wouldn't be any new manna to gather on that day. When the Sabbath came, the manna the people had saved overnight was still fresh and fine to eat. "It's not spoiled at all!" the people said.

For as long as the Israelites traveled and camped in the wilderness before they entered the Promised Land, God sent them manna. He knew what His people needed, and He took care of them.

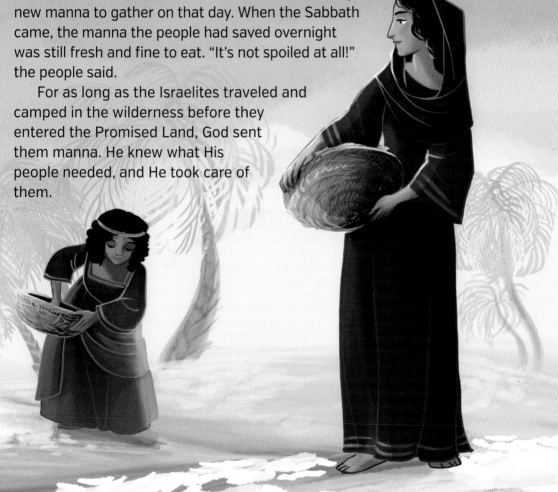

WHAT DOES IT MEAN?

When summer ends and school begins, you get a list of the school supplies you will need for your new class—things like crayons, markers, paper, and glue. But you can't get those things yourself. A grown-up buys them for you. Parents and grandparents love you and provide the school supplies you need.

One of God's names in the Bible is *The LORD Will Provide*. God loves us and knows exactly what we need. He promises to provide for us, and He does! When we are young, God gives the job of providing for us to our parents. When we grow up, He helps us work and earn money so we can buy the things we need. Sometimes when we need help, God sends a friend to help us, or He provides what we need with a miracle! God's gifts to us are always exactly right.

Dear God, I'm glad You always know what I need! Thank You for all the ways You provide for me. I love You, God. Amen.

LEARN MORE

- God also provided water in the wilderness for His people—from a rock! You can read about it in Exodus 17:1–7.
- First Timothy 6:17 says, "God . . . richly provides us with everything to enjoy."

WHAT HAPPENED NEXT?

Before they entered the Promised Land, the Israelites needed to learn how to live as God's people. So God came down in a great, thundering cloud to tell His people how they should live . . .

Meeting with God

God, the Holy One, says, "Can you compare me to anyone?"
—Isaiah 40:25 ICB

FROM EXODUS 19–20; 24–31; 35–40. Three months after God rescued the Israelites from Egypt, He told Moses to give His people a message: "You have seen how I take care of you. Obey Me and be My special people." The people agreed. Then God said to Moses, "On the third day, I will come down on the mountain and visit My people. Tell everyone to get ready!"

Whoosh, wash, splash, shake! All throughout their camp in the wilderness, the Israelites scrubbed their clothes and hung them up to dry. "Isn't this exciting?" one person asked another. "I wonder what will happen when God visits us!"

God is perfect and good in every way. He never does anything wrong.

On the morning of the third day, the people stood near Mount Sinai in their clean clothes. They heard thunder and a loud trumpet blast. They saw lightning in the sky and a thick cloud on the mountain. The mountain shook and the cloud smoked when God came down on the mountain in fire. Then the Israelites heard God's voice speaking to Moses and to them.

"I am the LORD, who brought you out of Egypt," God said. "Worship only Me. Never make or worship idols. Speak My name wisely. Rest on the Sabbath day, and honor your parents. Don't kill people. Be faithful to your husband or wife. Don't steal. Don't lie. Don't be jealous of what others have."

The thunder and lightning, trumpet and smoke frightened the people. But Moses said, "Don't be afraid! God wants you to honor Him. That's why He has come to give you these rules."

Then Moses again went up on the mountain to hear more from God. He wrote down God's rules and read them aloud to the people.

God's rules showed the Israelites how special God is. They agreed with Him again and said, "All that the LORD has told us, we will do!"

Not long after this, God gave Moses instructions for making a beautiful worship tent called the tabernacle. "Tell all the people with willing hearts to bring gifts," God said. "Here is what they can bring: gold, silver, and bronze. Red, blue, and purple thread. Linen, leather, acacia wood, olive oil, spices, and jewels. I will show you how to use these gifts for making a tent where I can live among My people."

People gladly brought their gifts, and soon the work began. God told Moses how to build the tabernacle and all the items to go with it. These included a golden lampstand, an altar, and a special box called the ark of the covenant, which reminded the people that God was with them.

When the work was done, God told Moses how to set up the tabernacle. Then the cloud that led the Israelites through the wilderness covered the tabernacle as the greatness of the Lord filled it.

WHAT DOES IT MEAN?

When a gymnast makes no mistakes in an event, we say she scored a perfect ten. When a baseball pitcher strikes out every batter, we say he threw a perfect game.

People can sometimes *do* certain things perfectly, but we can never *be* perfect because we sin—we do things that are wrong. But God is perfect—*holy*—all the time. God is good, loving, kind, merciful, powerful, and just. He never does anything wrong.

We cheer when we watch a gymnast score a perfect ten or a pitcher throw a perfect game. We can cheer for our perfect, holy God too. One of His names is *Holy One*. There's no one else like Him!

Dear God, I love You and trust You because You are holy—perfect and good. There's no one else like You! Amen.

LEARN MORE

Isaiah 6:3 says, "Holy, holy, holy is the LORD of hosts; the whole earth is full of his glory!"

WHAT HAPPENED NEXT?

Moses sent twelve scouts into the Promised Land. After forty days, ten of the scouts said it would be too hard to take over the land, but two scouts reminded the people that God had promised to give the land to them. The Israelites listened to the ten scouts and refused to go into the land, so God sent them back to the wilderness to live for forty years. And then . . .

Seven Times Around

And Moses built an altar and called the name of it, The LORD Is My Banner.
—Exodus 17:15

FROM JOSHUA 5–6. After Moses died, Joshua became the leader of the Israelites. He led them across the Jordan River and into the Promised Land as God told him to. *Now what?* Joshua wondered. *How do we go farther into the land from here?* The city of Jericho—with its tall, strong walls made of stone—stood in their way.

One day, Joshua looked up and saw a man standing nearby with a sword in his hand. "Are you for us or for Jericho?" Joshua asked.

"Neither," came the reply. "I am the commander of the Lord's army."

Joshua knew this was an angel from God! "What is your message?" Joshua asked.

"Take off your sandals, Joshua," the angel said. "You are standing on holy ground."

Joshua obeyed, and then he listened to God's instructions about the city of Jericho. "For six days," the angel said, "march around the city every day with all the soldiers. Carry the ark of the covenant with you. Seven priests will march in front of the ark, each carrying a trumpet. On the seventh day, march around the city seven times and then shout. The walls of the city of Jericho will fall down."

What a strange way to win a battle! But Joshua obeyed. He gave God's instructions to the people. The priests lined up in front of the ark. Then soldiers lined up ahead of the priests and behind the ark as well.

God leads us and helps us when we depend on Him.

"Let's go!" Joshua said. "But be quiet—no talking, not even a word, until the day I tell you to shout!" Joshua and the priests and the soldiers marched around the city, but no one said a word. Then they all went back to their camp.

The next morning, Joshua and the priests and the soldiers lined up again and marched around Jericho for a second time. They did this every day for six days.

But on the seventh day, Joshua and the priests and the soldiers lined up and marched around Jericho *seven* times. Then Joshua cried, "Shout!" and they all yelled as loud as they could.

As soon as the people shouted, the walls of Jericho began to shake. The people heard a *rumble* and a *roar.* Then the tall, strong walls of Jericho tumbled to the ground. Hurrah!

When the Israelites followed God's instructions and depended on Him, He gave them victory. Now they could keep going into the Promised Land.

Dear God, I will trust You to lead me like a banner. I'm glad I can follow You! Thank You, God. Amen.

WHAT DOES IT MEAN?

Have you ever watched a parade? Did you see any flags?

In a parade, marching bands and floats often carry flags or follow behind big signs called banners that tell us who they are and where they are from. Sometimes the people watching a parade wave flags too—maybe the flag of their school or the country where they live. When we carry a banner or wave a flag, we are telling other people whom we belong to and whom we follow. One of God's names in the Bible is *The LORD My Banner*. God is our banner when we follow Him, depend on Him, and help others know Him.

Joshua and the Israelites didn't have a banner to wave when they marched around Jericho. But they followed God's instructions and depended on Him to make the walls of Jericho fall down—and that is just what happened! King Solomon wrote, "His banner over me is love" (Song of Songs 2:4 ICB). With God as our banner, we know that our loving, good, and powerful God is helping us do what He wants us to do.

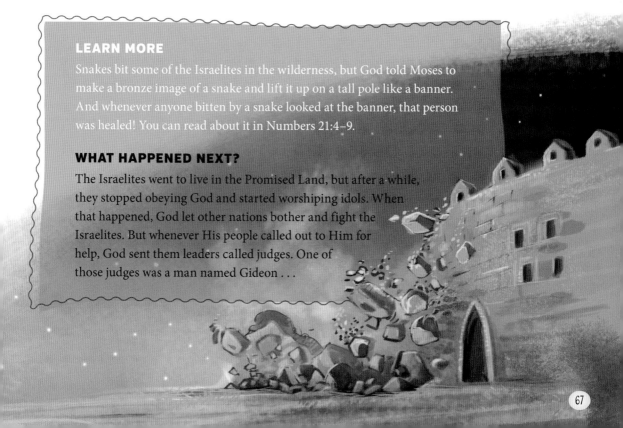

LEARN MORE

Snakes bit some of the Israelites in the wilderness, but God told Moses to make a bronze image of a snake and lift it up on a tall pole like a banner. And whenever anyone bitten by a snake looked at the banner, that person was healed! You can read about it in Numbers 21:4–9.

WHAT HAPPENED NEXT?

The Israelites went to live in the Promised Land, but after a while, they stopped obeying God and started worshiping idols. When that happened, God let other nations bother and fight the Israelites. But whenever His people called out to Him for help, God sent them leaders called judges. One of those judges was a man named Gideon . . .

THE LORD IS PEACE
Jehovah Shalom (jeh-HO-vuh sha-*LOME*)

Surprised by an Angel

Then Gideon built an altar there to the LORD and called it, The LORD Is Peace.
—Judges 6:24

FROM JUDGES 6–7. The Israelites had promised to obey God, but they didn't keep their promise. They stopped worshiping Him only, and they began to worship idols. So God allowed the people of other lands to fight with them and cause them trouble.

The people of Midian came with their camels and livestock and camped in tents throughout Israel. They ate all the crops the Israelites planted. The Israelites left their homes and went to hide in the mountains in dens and caves. Finally, they cried out to God and asked God for help.

One day, while Gideon was trying to hide some wheat from the Midianites, he suddenly saw someone who said to him, "The Lord is with you, mighty man!"

Gideon felt small, not mighty at all! "If God is with us," he asked, "why have all these bad things been happening to us? We need God to help us."

Everything good comes from God.

"I am sending you to save your people from the Midianites," the visitor said. It was the angel of the Lord!

"How can *I* save Israel?" Gideon wanted to know.

"God will be with you," the angel said.

"Can you show me a sign that this is true?" Gideon asked. "Now please wait here while I go and get a gift for you."

The angel waited while Gideon cooked a meal of meat, bread, and broth.

When Gideon brought him the food, the angel said, "Put the meat and bread on this rock, and pour the broth over it."

Gideon did what the angel said. Then the angel touched the food with the tip of his staff. *Pssst!* Fire sprang up from the rock. The food was gone—and so was the angel!

"It really was God's angel talking to me!" Gideon said, feeling afraid.

God answered him, "Don't worry, Gideon. Be at peace." Gideon built an altar to the Lord and called it The LORD Is Peace.

God told Gideon, "Pull down the altars built for idols." Gideon obeyed God, but he did it at night because he was afraid of his family and the people of his town. They were angry, but God protected him.

Then Gideon called for men to gather with him to fight the Midianites, and many Israelites came. "There are too many," God said. "This is My battle, not yours." God chose just three hundred men.

Gideon divided the men into three groups surrounding the Midianites' camp. He gave each man a trumpet and a torch inside a clay jar. When Gideon blew his trumpet, all the soldiers blew theirs too and smashed their jars so the torches could be seen. Instead of fighting with the Israelites, the frightened Midianites ran away!

Dear God, I'm glad You forgive me and help me and give me peace. Thank You for Jesus! Amen.

WHAT DOES IT MEAN?

Have you ever tried to work a puzzle with pieces missing? How did you feel when you couldn't finish the puzzle? Later, if you found the missing pieces and finished the puzzle, how did you feel?

When you finish a puzzle, it is *whole*. The picture in the puzzle is how it should be. Peace is a feeling of being *whole*. God wants to fill in our missing pieces, make us whole, and give us peace. One of God's names in the Bible is *The LORD Is Peace*.

When we do something we know is wrong, we don't have peace. But because Jesus died for our sins, God forgives us and gives us peace.

Sometimes, like Gideon, we may have a problem that worries or frightens us. Maybe someone in your family is sick, or maybe you have a hard spelling test coming up, or maybe someone at your school is a bully. But because God is with you and helping you, you can have peace. Jesus said, "My peace I give to you" [John 14:27].

LEARN MORE

Galatians 5:22–23 says, "The Spirit gives love, joy, peace, patience, kindness, goodness, faithfulness, gentleness, self-control" (ICB).

WHAT HAPPENED NEXT?

During the years when God sent judges to lead Israel, a Moabite woman named Ruth moved to Bethlehem with her mother-in-law, Naomi. They had nothing, but Ruth trusted God to take care of them . . .

GOD OF ALL COMFORT
El Nehkumah (EL neh-ku-*MAH*)

Sad, Then Happy

Blessed be the God and Father of our Lord Jesus Christ, the Father of mercies and God of all comfort.
—2 Corinthians 1:3

FROM THE BOOK OF RUTH. Ruth, from the land of Moab, stood on a dusty road near her mother-in-law, Naomi, an Israelite. Their husbands had died, and Naomi was going back to her home in Bethlehem.

"I want to go with you!" Ruth said. "Where you go, I will go. Where you live, I will live. Your people will be my people, and your God will be my God."

Naomi saw that Ruth was determined to go with her, so the two of them walked to Bethlehem together. But when they arrived, Naomi told people, "Don't call me Naomi anymore. Call me Mara. I was happy when I left, but now I am coming back sad."

Because the women were poor and had no husbands or sons to provide for them, Ruth went out to the barley field to pick up grain that fell to the ground as the barley was harvested. She worked in the field that belonged to a man named Boaz.

Boaz noticed Ruth working hard. "Who is that young woman?" he asked his servant.

"Her name is Ruth," the servant said. "She is from Moab. She came to Bethlehem with Naomi."

Boaz went to Ruth and said, "I've heard how kind you have been to Naomi and how you have helped her. You may always work in my field, and no one will bother you. You will have plenty of grain for Naomi and yourself."

When Ruth went back to Naomi's house that day, she told Naomi about meeting Boaz.

"God has remembered me!" Naomi said. "Boaz is a relative. God is taking good care of us!"

After the barley harvest came the wheat harvest. Ruth worked in Boaz's field every day. At the end of the wheat harvest, Naomi said, "It's time for you to marry again, Ruth." Naomi had an idea about who Ruth's new husband would be. And Naomi was right! Soon Boaz and Ruth were married, and then they had a baby boy and named him Obed.

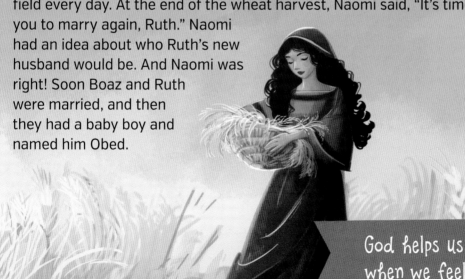

God helps us when we feel sad.

Naomi laughed with joy. She loved baby Obed and took care of him. The women of Bethlehem told Naomi, "God is so good! He has given you a new life and a wonderful daughter-in-law to look after you, and now He has given you a grandson!"

When Obed grew up, he had a son named Jesse. And when Jesse grew up, he became the father of Israel's great King David.

WHAT DOES IT MEAN?

Have you ever had a special blanket or stuffed animal to sleep with? When you are sick, is there a special food you like to eat? Or do you like for someone to put a cool cloth on your forehead or sing to you? When you are feeling sad, do you like someone to give you a back rub or a hug? Blankies and favorite foods and back rubs give us comfort. They help us feel better.

God gives us comfort too. One of His names is the *God of All Comfort*. Sometimes God uses people to help us feel better. They might pray for us or do something kind for us. Sometimes God surprises us with new friends and family members—as He did for Naomi and Ruth. And sometimes God uses His words in the Bible to comfort us.

God can use us to comfort other people too! Is there someone you can comfort today? Do something kind for that person, and tell him or her, "God loves you!"

Dear God, thank You for all the ways You comfort me! Show me how I can comfort someone else too. Amen.

LEARN MORE

When the prophet Elijah needed comfort, God gave him special food and then met him outside a cave and talked with him. You can read about it in 1 Kings 19:4–13.

WHAT HAPPENED NEXT?

During the time of the judges, the Philistines were one of the groups that fought against the Israelites. But the idol the Philistines worshiped couldn't stand up to God . . .

The Statue That Couldn't Stand Up

The LORD, whose very name is Jealous, is a God who is jealous about his relationship with you.
—Exodus 34:14 NLT

FROM 1 SAMUEL 4–7. Whenever the Israelites forgot about God and worshiped idols, God allowed trouble to come to them. When the Israelites went out to fight the Philistines, they lost the first battle.

"Why did God let us lose the fight?" the leaders of Israel wondered. But they didn't ask God why, and they didn't ask for His help. Instead, they decided to bring the ark of the covenant, God's special box in the tabernacle, to be with them in their camp. Everyone shouted so loudly when they saw the ark that the Philistines heard them and wondered what was happening.

When the Philistines realized that God's special box was in the Israelites' camp, they were afraid. "We know about God's power and how He rescued the Israelites from Egypt," they said. "We must really fight hard now!" So they fought with all their might and defeated the Israelites a second time.

Even worse, the Philistines captured the ark of the covenant! They took it to the city of Ashdod in their own land, to the temple of one of their idols, called Dagon. They set the ark next to a statue of Dagon.

God is the only true God. He wants us to worship Him only.

The next morning, the Philistines went into Dagon's temple again. "Oh no!" they cried. "Dagon fell down!" The statue of Dagon had fallen on its face in front of the ark of the covenant! They stood the statue back up. But the next morning, what did they see? The statue of Dagon had fallen in front of God's special box again! This time the idol had lost its hands and its head—they were lying in the doorway to the temple. No idol could stand before the power of the one true God!

The people of Ashdod also began to get sick. They were afraid of the ark of the covenant and asked their leaders, "What should we do?"

"Send the ark to the city of Gath," the leaders said.

But the people of Gath got sick too and sent the ark to the city of Ekron. When the people of Ekron saw the ark of the covenant, they said, "Send the ark back where it belongs!"

Finally, the leaders agreed. They put God's special box on a cart drawn by two cows and sent it off. The cows took the cart with the ark straight back to the Israelites!

At that time, God's prophet Samuel was leading the Israelites. "Are you ready to serve the Lord with all your hearts?" Samuel asked the people. "Then stop worshiping idols. Serve God only, and He will deliver you from the fighting Philistines."

WHAT DOES IT MEAN?

There are two ways to be jealous—a bad way and a good way. The bad way is when you want what other people have, maybe their clothes or their games or their talent at sports. You want what someone else has so much that you can't even be friends with that person. You are jealous of him or her.

But that is not what the name *Jealous God* means. God is jealous in the good way—He watches out for us. He wants *us* to have good things in our lives, and the best thing He wants us to have is His love. He doesn't want His people to wander off and worship anything or anyone else. He knows that isn't good for us.

Clothes and games and sports are good, but God wants us to remember what is most important—loving and serving Him!

Dear God, thank You for always wanting what is good for me! Help me remember to worship You only. I love You, God. Amen.

LEARN MORE

When the apostle Paul went to Athens, he saw that the people there worshiped many idols. He told them about the one true God! You can read about it in Acts 17:16–31.

WHAT HAPPENED NEXT?

The Israelites wanted a human king because the other nations around them had human kings. God gave them what they wanted. He chose Saul to be their first king, but Saul did not obey God with all his heart, and he did not make a good king. So God chose someone else to be king after Saul . . .

A Shepherd for a King

The LORD is my shepherd.
—Psalm 23:1

FROM 1 SAMUEL 16–17; PSALM 23. David, the youngest son of Jesse, lived in Bethlehem. He had seven older brothers. Three of them were soldiers in King Saul's army, but David tended his father's sheep.

"This way, little sheep!" David called, and his sheep twitched their ears. They recognized David's voice.

Baa-baa! answered the sheep. They nudged each other as they gathered together and followed David. He always took them somewhere good!

Sometimes David took the sheep to a sunny pasture with delicious green grass for them to eat. He found quiet streams of clear water where they could safely drink. And on hot days, he found cool, shady places where the sheep could lie down, chew their cud, and take a nap. David rubbed their noses with oil first to keep the flies away.

While the sheep rested, David played his lyre and sang to them. David loved God, and all his life he wrote and sang songs to God to praise Him. One of David's songs begins like this:

> The Lord is my shepherd.
>   I have everything I need.
> He gives me rest in green pastures.
>   He leads me to calm water.
> He gives me new strength. (Psalm 23:1–3 ICB)

God cares for the people who love Him the way a good shepherd cares for his sheep.

Wild animals sometimes roamed through the countryside where David tended his sheep. Sometimes David had to fight off a hungry lion or bear looking for a lamb to eat. He would save the lamb and bring it back to the flock. At night, David kept his flock safe in a fenced-in space, with a fire to keep wild animals away.

One day, God told the prophet Samuel to go to Bethlehem to see Jesse, David's father. "The next king of Israel will be one of Jesse's sons," God said. Samuel traveled to Bethlehem and invited Jesse and his sons to a feast.

When Samuel saw Jesse's son Eliab, he thought, *This must be the one God has chosen.* But God said, "No, he is not the one. Eliab is handsome, but I don't judge by how someone looks. I care about the heart—how someone thinks and acts."

Samuel met six more brothers. "God hasn't chosen any of these," he told Jesse. "Are all your sons here?"

"There is one more, the youngest," Jesse said. "He is out in the fields, keeping the sheep."

"Send for him and bring him here," Samuel said. "We won't eat the feast until he comes."

Jesse sent for David, and when David came in, God told Samuel, "This is the one." Samuel poured oil over David's head as a sign that David would be the next king of Israel.

Dear God, You are the best shepherd I could ever have! Thank You for taking care of me the way a good shepherd takes care of sheep. Amen.

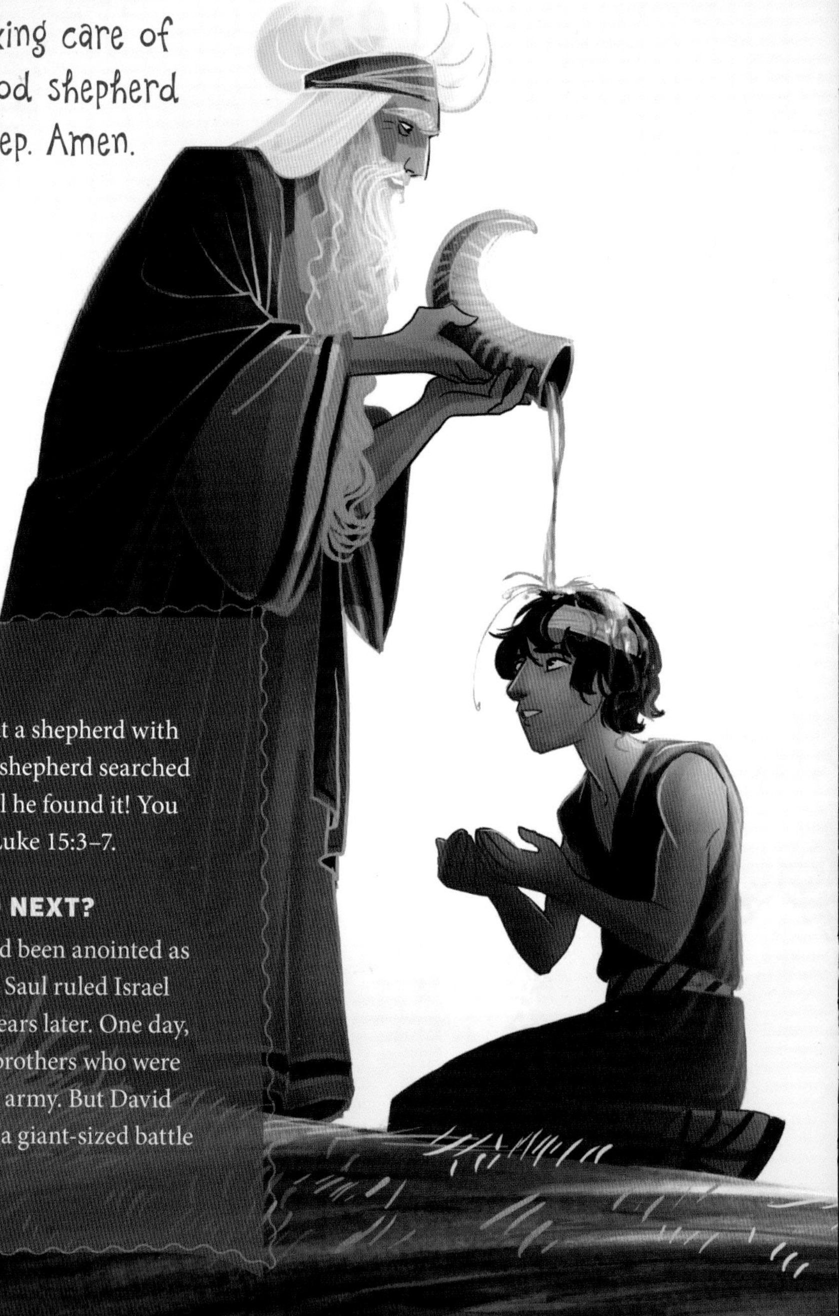

LEARN MORE

Jesus told a story about a shepherd with a hundred sheep. The shepherd searched for one lost sheep until he found it! You can read the story in Luke 15:3–7.

WHAT HAPPENED NEXT?

Even though David had been anointed as the next king of Israel, Saul ruled Israel until he died, fifteen years later. One day, David went to see his brothers who were fighting in King Saul's army. But David soon found himself in a giant-sized battle of his own . . .

WHAT DOES IT MEAN?

Have you ever seen sheep? They aren't very good at taking care of themselves. They can get into trouble quickly. Sheep need a shepherd!

Sometimes people are like sheep. We can get into trouble quickly, and we need a shepherd! One of God's names is *The LORD My Shepherd*. David learned that how a good shepherd cares for sheep is a lot like how God cares for us.

God provides what we need, just as a shepherd provides good grass and clean water for his sheep. God shows us how to live and the right paths to follow. He watches over us, and if we wander away from Him, He looks for us and brings us back. He protects us just as a shepherd protects his sheep from wild animals.

Jesus said, "My sheep hear my voice . . . and they follow me" [John 10:27].

With a Stone and a Sling

The Lord is my strength and shield. I trust him, and he helps me.
—Psalm 28:7 ICB

FROM 1 SAMUEL 17. Israel's soldiers shivered in their boots. Across the valley in front of them camped the army of the Philistines. And one of the Philistine soldiers, Goliath, looked like a giant—he was more than nine feet tall! He wore heavy armor and carried a big spear.

"Send someone out to fight me!" Goliath yelled to the Israelites, every day for forty days. "Come on!"

The Israelites trembled. No one wanted to fight Goliath.

Then David, the son of Jesse, came into the Israelite camp with supplies for his brothers. While he was there, he saw and heard Goliath.

"Send someone out to fight me!" Goliath yelled again.

"That giant is defying the army of God!" David said. "Who is going to fight him?"

But none of the soldiers—and not even King Saul—wanted to fight Goliath.

"I will fight Goliath," David told the king.

"How can you do that?" the king asked. "You're just a boy." "I have fought with lions and bears to save my father's sheep," David said. "And God will help me fight this giant." "Wear my armor, then," the king told David. David put on the king's armor, but he took it off again. "I can't wear this," he said. "I'm not used to it." Instead, he chose five smooth stones from a nearby brook and put them in his shepherd's pouch. Then, with his sling in his hand, David walked toward Goliath.

When we are weak, God is strong.

"What?" yelled Goliath. "A boy is coming to fight me? Ha-ha, ha-ha, HA!"

"I come against you in the name of the Lord, the God of the armies of Israel, whom you have challenged and insulted!" David yelled back. "Today everyone will know there is a God in Israel and that He saves—but not with swords and spears! The battle is the Lord's!"

David put a stone in his sling and twirled the sling as he ran toward Goliath. The stone flew out of the sling and hit Goliath in the forehead. Down he went, falling on his face!

The army of the Philistines turned and ran away. Then Israel's army gave a big shout and chased after them as they ran.

WHAT DOES IT MEAN?

Have you ever watched ants at work? Most ants are very tiny, but they are strong! Ants can carry loads bigger and heavier than they are. Why are ants so strong? Because that is the way God designed their bodies.

Our bodies can be strong too if we exercise our muscles and eat healthy foods. But being strong isn't just about muscles. It's also about being brave and doing the right thing, even when that's hard.

One of God's names is *The Lord My Strength*. Sometimes God gives us a job we think we can't do—it seems too hard for us. Sometimes we are tired or sick and feel weak, but God is always strong. God gives us the power we need. He is our strength every day.

LEARN MORE

Philippians 4:13 says, "I can do all things through Christ because he gives me strength" (ICB).

WHAT HAPPENED NEXT?

When Saul died, David became king. He ruled for forty years. David wanted to build a temple for God in Jerusalem, but God told David his son Solomon would be the next king and would build the temple. When it was time for Solomon to become king, God had a surprise for him . . .

Dear God, thank You for being strong! I'm glad You are my strength every day. Amen.

Jehovah Ori (jeh-HO-vuh or-*EE*)

A Very Important Question

The LORD is my light.
—Psalm 27:1

FROM 1 KINGS 3–4. God chose David's son Solomon to be the next king. Solomon was a young man when he became king, just as his father had been.

One night, after he had been worshiping the Lord, Solomon fell asleep and began to dream. God appeared to him in his dream. "Ask Me for whatever you want," God told Solomon, "and I will give it to you."

What should I ask for? Solomon wondered. *Should I ask for a very long life, or to be rich, or to be famous?*

But Solomon didn't ask God for any of those things.

"You were loving and kind to my father, David," Solomon said, "because he loved and followed You. And You gave him a son to be king after him, and I am that son. But I am young and new at this, so please, give me wisdom. Give me understanding to know what is right and what is wrong, so I can be a good king to Your people."

Solomon's request pleased God. "I will give you wisdom," God said. "And I also will give you what you have not asked for—riches and honor. And if you obey Me all your days, I will give you a long life too."

The dream ended, and Solomon woke up. What an amazing dream! Solomon went to Jerusalem and worshiped God, and then he held a big feast for all his servants.

God kept His promises to Solomon. He made Solomon rich, and He made him the wisest man on earth. Solomon helped people solve problems. He wrote thousands of songs and proverbs. He learned about God's creation, including the trees, animals, birds, reptiles, and fish. Visitors from other lands traveled to Israel to honor King Solomon and listen to him because he was so wise.

God shows us how to have a good life.

WHAT DOES IT MEAN?

Crash! Boom! Sometimes a storm pulls down electric lines and the lights go out. Has your family ever had to get out candles or flashlights so that you could see in the dark? Without light, we can't see clearly. We need light to be able to get around safely.

Just as light shows us which way we should go in the dark, wisdom shows us what we should do. Because he wanted to be a good king, Solomon asked God for wisdom. We can ask God for wisdom too, and He will help us make good choices.

The wisdom God gives guides us each day, just as light guides us in the dark. One of God's names is *The LORD My Light*. God's words in the Bible teach us what is right and show us how to make good choices. God's words are the light that make us wise.

Dear God, thank You for flashlights and candles when it is dark, and thank You for giving me Your wisdom and light. Amen.

WHAT HAPPENED NEXT?

After Solomon died, Israel split into two kingdoms—Israel in the north and Judah in the south. Kings who would not obey God and worshiped idols led the people to disobey God too. God sent prophets to warn the people and call them to follow Him again, but the people would not. Elijah was one of the prophets sent to the Northern Kingdom. After him came Elisha. Then one day, Elisha told a man named Naaman to do something strange . . .

Who Can Help?

"I am the LORD who heals you."
—Exodus 15:26 NLT

FROM 2 KINGS 5. Naaman, the commander of the Syrian army, had a bad skin disease.

A young Israelite girl worked as a servant to Naaman's wife. "I wish Naaman could see God's prophet in Samaria of Israel," the girl said to her mistress. "The prophet would cure Naaman of his disease!"

When Naaman heard this, he went to see his friend, the king of Syria. "I have heard that I could be cured in the land of Israel," Naaman told the king.

"Then you must go there!" the king said. "I will send you to the king of Israel with a letter asking him to heal you."

Naaman and his servants traveled to Israel in chariots. They took gifts for the king of Israel, along with the letter from Naaman's king.

But the king of Israel didn't know how to make Naaman well! *What is the king of Syria thinking by sending Naaman to me?* he wondered.

The prophet Elisha heard that Naaman had come to see Israel's king. "Send Naaman to me," Elisha told the king. "He will learn about God's power."

So Naaman went to Elisha's house in his chariot. He got out and stood at the door and waited to see Elisha. But Elisha sent a messenger out to tell Naaman, "Go to the Jordan River and wash in it seven times. Then you will be cured of your skin disease."

"What?" Naaman yelled to his servants. "I thought Elisha would come out and heal me right away! Why would I wash in the muddy Jordan River? We have better rivers in our own land!" Naaman turned and walked away from Elisha's house. "Come on! We're going home!" he said.

God makes us well when we are sick or hurt.

"Wait, please," said Naaman's servants. "Elisha has asked you to do a very simple thing. If he had asked you to do a hard thing, you would do it. So why not do this simple thing and be healed?"

Naaman thought about that. "All right, then," he said. He went to the Jordan River. He waded in and dipped himself under the water—one, two, three, four, five, six, seven times!

Naaman looked at his skin. His servants looked too. Naaman's skin was like the skin of a brand-new baby! The skin disease was gone—just as the prophet said would happen if Naaman obeyed!

Naaman was well. God had healed him!

Dear God, You are my healer when I am hurt or sick. Thank You for doctors, nurses, and medicine and all the ways You heal me! Amen.

WHAT DOES IT MEAN?

When you get a cut or a scrape, what do you do? First, you wash the dirt and germs away with soap and water. Then your mom or dad puts some medicine and a bandage on it. Eventually, the cut will heal and be gone. New skin will grow where the scrape was.

If you get sick, what happens? Your mom and dad take care of you. They may take you to see the doctor and give you some medicine. Soon you are feeling better, ready to start playing again!

One of God's names is *The LORD Who Heals*. God made our bodies able to heal themselves in many ways when we are hurt or sick. Eating healthy food and getting exercise can help us get well and stay well. God also uses doctors and medicines to help our bodies heal. And sometimes, as He did for Naaman, He heals us right away! No matter how He does it, God is our healer.

LEARN MORE

Jesus healed many sick people, including a man with leprosy and the paralyzed servant of a Roman officer (Matthew 8) and a man born blind (John 9).

WHAT HAPPENED NEXT?

Because His people would not obey Him, God allowed other nations to fight with them. One of those nations was Syria. But God's people did not fight alone . . .

Angels All Around

The LORD of Heaven's Armies—he is the King of glory.
—Psalm 24:10 NLT

FROM 2 KINGS 6. The king of Syria began to fight the Israelites. But every time the Syrians planned a battle, the Israelites found out about it and went somewhere else.

"Who is telling the Israelites about our plans?" the king of Syria wanted to know. He couldn't figure it out, and it bothered him greatly. So the

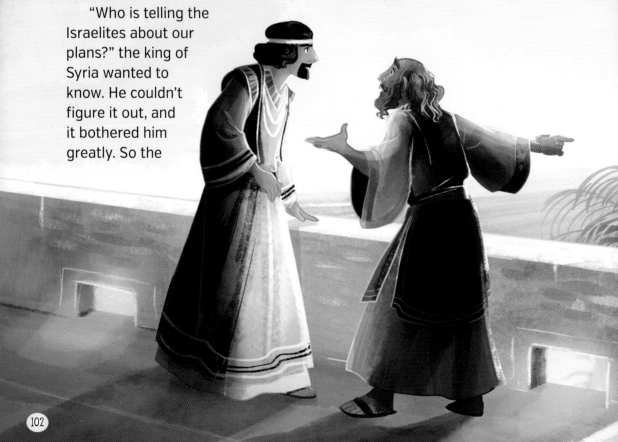

king called his servants and said, "Please tell me who among us is for the king of Israel instead of for us! How can we surprise the Israelites with a battle if someone keeps telling them where we are?"

"None of us is the problem," the king's servants told him. "But Elisha, God's prophet in Israel, knows your plans and tells them to Israel's king."

"Well, then," the king of Syria said, "go find out where this Elisha is. Then I can send soldiers to capture him."

The servants searched for Elisha. "We have learned that Elisha is in the city of Dothan," they told the king. So the king sent a great army with many horses and chariots, and they surrounded the city of Dothan.

In the morning, when Elisha's servant went outside, he saw the Syrian army everywhere he looked. Soldiers with horses and chariots circled the city. "Oh no!" Elisha's servant cried. "What are we going to do?"

Elisha came outside and saw the army too. "Don't be afraid," Elisha said. "Those who are with us are more than those who are with them."

Elisha's servant didn't see anyone with him and Elisha. Then Elisha prayed, "O Lord, please let my servant see what I can see."

God reigns over everything, on earth and in heaven.

God answered Elisha's prayer. Suddenly, the servant could see what Elisha saw—an army of angels, horses, and chariots of fire covered the mountain and surrounded Elisha and his servant! They had been there all along, sent by God to protect Elisha from the enemy king.

When the Syrian army came down on the town, looking for Elisha, Elisha prayed again. "O Lord, make them blind," he said. And God did. He confused the Syrian soldiers, and they let Elisha lead them right to the king of Israel. The soldiers never knew it was Elisha or that he was leading them to Israel's king!

When they reached the king, Elisha prayed for God to let them see again. Then he told the king, "Give them something to eat, and send them back to their master."

So the king of Israel threw a big feast and then sent the soldiers away. Syria didn't bother Israel again for a long time!

Dear God, even though I can't see You or Your angel armies, I know You are there, watching over me, and I'm glad! Amen.

WHAT DOES IT MEAN?

In the Chronicles of Narnia books by C. S. Lewis, there are two worlds. When the children are in the professor's house, standing in front of the wardrobe, they can't see Narnia. But after they go into the wardrobe and discover it, they know Narnia is always there.

We can't see heaven, God, or the angels in heaven, but they are real and always there. God rules over both what we can see and what we can't see. He is *The LORD of Heaven's Armies*. Elisha's servant didn't need to be afraid—and neither do we—because God commands a heavenly army that fights for us and protects us when we need help.

LEARN MORE

Psalm 46:7 says, "The Lord of heaven's armies is with us. The God of Jacob is our protection" (ICB).

WHAT HAPPENED NEXT?

God's people refused to turn back to God and worship Him only. So God allowed other nations to take His people captive. The Northern Kingdom fell to the Assyrians, and later the Southern Kingdom fell to the Babylonians. A man named Daniel was taken captive, but he chose to worship only God, no matter what happened . . .

THE LORD MY SHIELD

Jehovah Magen (jeh-HO-vuh mah-gih-*NEE*)

Safe from Hungry Lions

He is our help and our shield.
—Psalm 33:20

FROM DANIEL 6. Daniel, one of the Jewish exiles in Babylon, served the rulers of Babylon his whole life. When Darius became king, he put Daniel and two other high officials in charge of all the workers who collected money for the king's treasury.

Daniel did such a good job and served with such a good spirit that Darius planned to put him in charge of the whole kingdom. That made the other high officials jealous. They wanted to find a reason to get rid

106

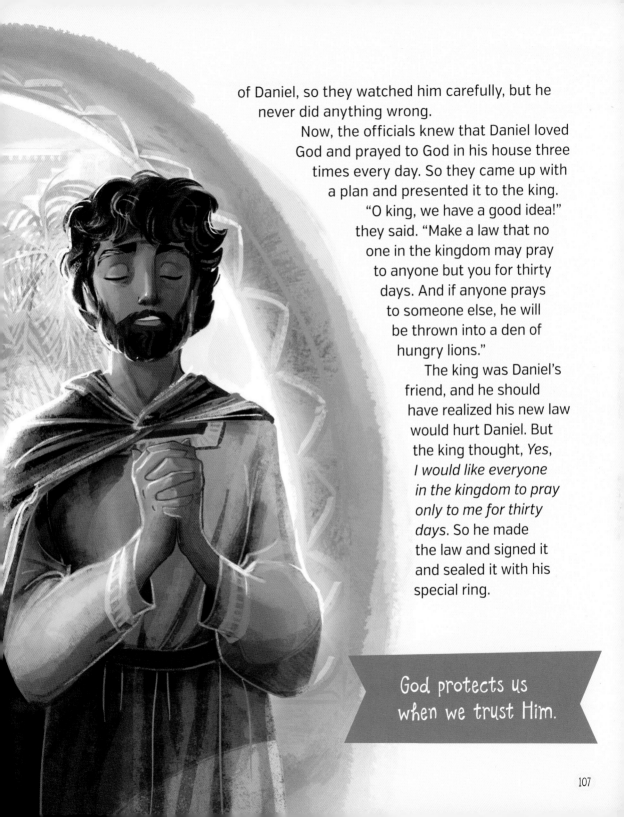

of Daniel, so they watched him carefully, but he never did anything wrong.

Now, the officials knew that Daniel loved God and prayed to God in his house three times every day. So they came up with a plan and presented it to the king.

"O king, we have a good idea!" they said. "Make a law that no one in the kingdom may pray to anyone but you for thirty days. And if anyone prays to someone else, he will be thrown into a den of hungry lions."

The king was Daniel's friend, and he should have realized his new law would hurt Daniel. But the king thought, *Yes, I would like everyone in the kingdom to pray only to me for thirty days.* So he made the law and signed it and sealed it with his special ring.

God protects us when we trust Him.

Daniel heard about the new law, but he didn't stop praying to God because praying to God was the right thing to do. He went to his house, knelt by the window, and prayed to God three times every day, just as he had always done.

The other officials spied on Daniel and saw what he was doing. Then they hurried to tell the king.

King Darius was very worried and upset. "What have I done?" he said. "There must be a way I can help Daniel instead of throwing him into a den of hungry lions!"

But even the king could not change a law once it was written. With great sadness, the king sent for Daniel. "May your God, whom you always serve, deliver you!" the king said. Then the king's servants threw Daniel into the den of hungry lions and placed a big stone over the top.

The king went back to his palace, but he couldn't eat or sleep. In the morning, at the first light, he hurried back to the lions' den. As he got close, he called out, "Daniel, servant of the living God, has your God saved you?"

Would Daniel answer him? Would he hear Daniel's voice?
Yes!

"O king," Daniel answered, "God sent an angel to close the lions' mouths, and they have not hurt me!"

"Wonderful, wonderful!" said the king. He ordered his servants to pull Daniel out of the lions' den right away.

Then the king made a new law. "Everyone in the kingdom must honor Daniel's God, for He is the living God who has saved Daniel from the power of the lions."

WHAT DOES IT MEAN?

If you forget sunscreen at the pool or the beach, or if you stay in the sun too long, you get a sunburn—and it hurts! *Ow!* But sunscreen and a big umbrella shield you from the harmful rays of the sun that could hurt you.

Long ago, soldiers carried shields. In a battle, they held their shields in front of them to knock away arrows and other weapons used against them.

God's enemy, Satan, sometimes makes bad things happen and tries to get us to do wrong things. But one of God's names is *The Lord My Shield.* God keeps us safe from what might hurt us, and He tells us to knock away the enemy's darts and arrows with our trust in Him. "Hold up the shield of faith to stop the fiery arrows of the devil" [Ephesians 6:16 NLT].

Dear God, help me to trust You always. Thank You for being my shield! Amen.

LEARN MORE

Psalm 3:3 says, "Lord, you are my shield. You are my wonderful God who gives me courage" (ICB).

WHAT HAPPENED NEXT?

After seventy years as captives, the people from the Southern Kingdom of Judah were allowed to return to Jerusalem to rebuild the temple. Later, they rebuilt the city walls too. And when the right time came, God would keep His promise to send Someone—Jesus—to make everything right again . . .

Stories from the New Testament

Good News!

"They shall call his name Immanuel" (which means, God with us).
—Matthew 1:23

FROM MATTHEW 1; LUKE 1–2. Long ago, before He made the world, God made a wonderful plan. At just the right time, He would send Someone to help all the people of the world. God promised He would do this. Some people believed God, and they waited patiently. Some people forgot about God's promise.

But God always keeps His promises!

One day, God sent the angel Gabriel to the town of Nazareth with a message for Mary, a young woman engaged to marry a man named Joseph.

"Hello, favored one!" Gabriel said. "The Lord is with you!"

Oh! Mary had never seen an angel before! Why had he come? What was he talking about?

"Don't be afraid, Mary," Gabriel said. "God is pleased with you. You are going to have a special baby boy, and you must name Him Jesus. He will be very great, and He will be called the Son of God. He will reign over God's kingdom forever."

"I am not married yet, so how will this happen?" Mary asked.

"God's power will cause it," Gabriel said. "The baby will be holy—the Son of God. Nothing is impossible with God."

"I will do whatever God wants," Mary said. "So let this amazing thing take place, just as you have said."

The angel also appeared to Joseph, in a dream. "Mary's baby is from God," Gabriel told Joseph. "Take care of her while she is waiting for the baby to be born." Joseph obeyed.

Then, before the baby was born, the Roman emperor made a new law: everyone living in his empire must be registered and counted.

"I know this is a bad time for you to travel, Mary dear," Joseph said. "But we have to obey the emperor. We must go to Bethlehem, my hometown, to be counted."

While Mary and Joseph were in Bethlehem, the time came for Mary's baby to be born—a sweet, beautiful baby boy. Mary wrapped Him in swaddling cloths to keep Him warm and cozy.

Jesus is with us.

But all the rooms in the Bethlehem inn had been filled by other travelers. So where did the baby Jesus sleep? Mary laid baby Jesus in a manger, an animals' feeding trough, filled with hay. Then she and Joseph rested and took care of the baby and kept Him safe.

WHAT DOES IT MEAN?

If a storm with loud thunder and lightning wakes you up, do you run to find your mom and dad or climb in bed with your sister or brother? Sometimes we don't want to be alone—we want somebody else to be with us!

One of Jesus' names is *Immanuel*, which means "God with us." God came to live with people on earth when Jesus was born! Jesus came to show us that God loves us and doesn't want us to be alone! So even in the middle of a storm, we don't ever have to feel alone or afraid—God is with us!

Dear God, I'm so glad You want to be with us! Thank You for sending Jesus to show us Your love. Amen.

LEARN MORE

Do you remember reading about Joshua and the battle of Jericho? When Joshua became the leader of the Israelites, God told him, "Don't be afraid. The Lord your God will be with you everywhere you go" (Joshua 1:9 ICB).

WHAT HAPPENED NEXT?

When Jesus was born, angels came to tell the news. Who heard the news first? Not the people you might expect . . .

The Shepherds' Surprise

God will give a son to us. . . . His name will be . . . Prince of Peace.
—Isaiah 9:6 ICB

FROM LUKE 2. While Mary fed baby Jesus in a stable in Bethlehem and Joseph held and rocked Him, sleepy shepherds watched over their flocks in fields outside the little town.

Suddenly, the dark fields lit up with the bright light of heaven!

Baa, baa, baa! The sheep woke up.

"What's going on?" the sleepy shepherds asked. "Someone is here! Who is it?"

Jesus gives us peace with God.

Standing near the shepherds was an angel! "Don't be afraid!" the angel said. "I've come with good news for you and all people. Today in Bethlehem, your Savior has been born. You will find Him wrapped in swaddling cloths and lying in a manger."

Amazing! thought the shepherds. They wondered why the angel had come to give *them* such good news. They were just dirty, smelly shepherds who stayed outside with their sheep. Everyone looked down on them—they couldn't even go into the temple to worship God.

Then the sky filled with angels who began to praise God together. "Glory to God!" they shouted. "And peace on earth to those who please Him!"

When the angels went back to heaven, the fields were dark and quiet again. "Let's go find that baby and see Him for ourselves!" the shepherds said. So they hurried to Bethlehem, searching for baby Jesus. What a sight they were, running through the dark streets! Then they spotted a light in a small stable, and they found Mary and Joseph and the baby there.

"It's just like the angel told us!" the shepherds said. "The baby is wrapped in swaddling cloths and lying in a manger!"

Mary and Joseph were surprised to see the shepherds. They were even more surprised to hear the shepherds tell them about the angels. "This baby is the One God has sent to be the Savior!" the shepherds said. "That's what the angel told us!"

The shepherds went back to their sheep, but they couldn't stop talking about everything that had happened. "What wonderful things we saw and heard tonight!" they said. "A special baby has been born, sent from God! And God sent angels to tell *us* the news and give *us* the message of peace!"

WHAT DOES IT MEAN?

Do you know the story of Cinderella? In that fairy tale, Cinderella's life is full of trouble until she meets the royal prince at a ball and marries him. Meeting the prince changes Cinderella's life completely.

One of Jesus' names is the *Prince of Peace*. When Jesus is our Savior, our sins are forgiven, and someday we will live with Him in heaven forever. Our future changes completely! This good news gives us peace with God, and God wants everyone—even sleepy, smelly shepherds—to know this good news.

Dear God, thank You for Jesus, the Prince of Peace. Thank You for giving me peace every day. Amen.

LEARN MORE

The prophet Isaiah wrote this about peace: "You will keep in perfect peace all who trust in you, all whose thoughts are fixed on you!" (Isaiah 26:3 NLT).

WHAT HAPPENED NEXT?

Wise men from the East came to worship Jesus while He was still a young child. Then Mary and Joseph took Jesus to Egypt to keep Him safe from a bad king named Herod. After Herod died, the family returned to Israel and settled in Nazareth, where Jesus grew up . . .

Like Father, Like Son

The child to be born will be called holy—the Son of God.
—Luke 1:35

FROM MATTHEW 3; MARK 1; LUKE 2–3. When He was little, Jesus watched and listened as Joseph sawed, hammered, and sanded to make things out of wood. When Jesus was older, He learned to make things out of wood too—tables and stools, lampstands and dishes.

At synagogue school, Jesus learned to read and recite Scripture. He loved God and God's words! When He was twelve, Jesus went with Mary and Joseph and their friends and family to celebrate the Passover Feast in Jerusalem.

After the feast, when it was time to go home, Jesus stayed behind. He talked to the teachers at the temple and asked them lots of questions. They asked Him questions too, and they were amazed by His answers.

Jesus shows us what God is like.

When Mary and Joseph realized Jesus wasn't with their family or friends on the road to Nazareth, they hurried back to Jerusalem to look for Him.

After a day of searching the city, they found Jesus in the temple. "Jesus, we have been so worried!" Mary said.

"Why were you looking for Me?" Jesus asked. "Didn't you know I needed to be in My Father's house?" But Jesus was obedient. He said good-bye to the temple teachers and went back to Nazareth with Mary and Joseph.

As the years went by, Jesus grew taller, and very wise. People enjoyed Him and thought well of Him. And God loved Him too.

Now, Jesus had a cousin named John. He grew up in the wilderness, wearing clothes made of camel's hair and eating locusts and wild honey. God had given John a special job: "Prepare the way for the Lord. Make the road straight for him" (Matthew 3:3 ICB). People came from all around to hear John preach, to confess their sins, and to be baptized in the Jordan River.

One day while John was baptizing, he looked up and saw Jesus coming toward him. "Why do *You* want to be baptized, Jesus?" John asked. John knew that Jesus had never done anything wrong. He knew that Jesus was God's Son. "I should be baptized by You instead," John said.

"We should do all the things that are right," Jesus said.

So John baptized Jesus, and God's Spirit came down from heaven like a dove and landed on Jesus. Then a voice from heaven, God's voice, said, "This is My Son, and I love Him! I am very pleased with Him!"

WHAT DOES IT MEAN?

Have you ever heard someone say "Oh, you look so much like your father!" or "You look more like your mother every day!"? Children often do look a lot like their parents.

No one knows what God looks like. But Jesus came and showed us what God is like by the things He said and did while He was on earth. That is one reason why Jesus is called the *Son of God*. He also is called the Son of God because Jesus *is* God! He has always existed with God.

God is Father, Son, and Holy Spirit. It's a mystery to us, but we know it is true.

LEARN MORE

- First John 4:9 says, "God showed how much he loved us by sending his one and only Son into the world so that we might have eternal life through him" (NLT).
- Jesus said, "I and the Father are one" (John 10:30).

WHAT HAPPENED NEXT?

After Jesus was baptized, He spent forty days in the wilderness, where He was tempted by Satan. Then He began to teach people about the kingdom of God, and He also healed the sick. As the news about Jesus spread, more and more people came to see Him . . . .

Dear God, thank You for sending Jesus to show us what You are like. Amen.

Up, Down, Up

"It is the sick who need a doctor. . . . I have come to invite sinners to change their hearts and lives!"
—Luke 5:31–32 ICB

FROM MATTHEW 9; MARK 2; LUKE 5. "Jesus is back in town!" people in Capernaum said to one another. "Let's go see Him!" They filled the house where Jesus was staying—people even stood outside the door, looking in. Teachers and leaders had come to listen to Jesus too.

Then four friends came to the house, carrying a man on a mat. The man was paralyzed—he couldn't walk. "Jesus can heal you," the four friends told the man. "We are taking you to see Jesus!"

But not one more person could get into the house! What would the four friends do now?

"The roof!" the friends said. "Let's go up the stairs to the roof. Careful. Go slow. Don't drop him!" When they got to the roof, the four friends laid down the man on his mat. "Whew! We did it!" they said.

Jesus heals and forgives.

But how would they get down to where Jesus was?

"We'll make a hole in the roof!" the friends said, and they started digging. The grass and mud that formed the roof gave way, and the friends could see into the house. They saw Jesus! The friends kept digging. Soon the hole in the roof was big enough for the man on the mat to fit through.

"Down you go!" the four friends said, and they let the man down through the hole in the roof on his mat—right in front of Jesus!

"Hello, friend!" Jesus said. He could see that the man and the four friends had great faith. "Your sins are forgiven."

Why did Jesus say that? wondered the teachers and leaders. *No one except God can forgive sins!*

Jesus knew what they were thinking. "Is it easier to forgive sins or to heal?" He asked. "But so you will know I have authority to do both—" He turned to the man on the mat and said, "Get up, pick up your mat, and go home."

What would happen? No one said a word.

Then the man on the mat got up! He picked up his mat. People near the door squeezed together to clear a path for him. The happy man walked out the door and headed for home, just as Jesus had told him to do.

"Wow!" people said. "Amazing! And wonderful! We have never seen anything like this before!"

Dear God, thank You for Jesus, our Great Physician. I'm glad He knows how to make me well. Amen.

WHAT DOES IT MEAN?

Doctors help us get well when we are sick. What is your doctor's name?

Men and women go to college and medical school for many years before they can be doctors. They also promise to always do what is best for the sick people who come to them for help.

Physician is another word for *doctor*. We call Jesus the *Great Physician* because He is the very best doctor. He didn't have to go to school to learn how to make people well. He can heal our bodies when they are sick—and He can forgive our sins—because He is God. He can make us well in every way!

LEARN MORE

When Jesus visited Peter's house, Peter's mother-in-law was sick.
You can read what Jesus did in Matthew 8:14–15.

WHAT HAPPENED NEXT?

Jesus continued to teach and to heal. He chose twelve followers to
become His special disciples. Great crowds followed Him wherever
He went, and He taught them many things . . .

Learning from Jesus

They said to him, "Rabbi" (which means Teacher), "where are you staying?"
—John 1:38

FROM MATTHEW 5–7; LUKE 6. When Jesus visited a town, He often went to the synagogue to teach about God. People loved to listen to Him, and crowds began to follow Him as He went from place to place.

One day Jesus went up on a mountainside and sat down. He called His disciples to Him and began to teach them. Everyone listened to what Jesus had to say.

Jesus taught about God's kingdom. "God blesses you when you depend on Him," He said, "and when you want what is right and good. So be kind and forgiving, and always follow God."

Jesus taught about helping others. "Let your light shine so others can find God and follow Him too," He said. "Give what you can to help those in need, but don't make a show of it. Don't give to get praise for yourself."

Jesus taught about how to treat enemies. "Love the people who are mean to you," He said, "because God loves every person. Pray for your enemies and do kind things for them."

Jesus taught about money. "Spend your money on what is good," He said. "Use it to help other people. Don't keep your money just for yourself. If you love God, you can't love money too."

Jesus taught about worry. "God takes care of all the flowers and the little birds," He said, "so He will certainly take care of you! You don't need to worry. Make God and His ways the most important things in your life. Then God will give you everything you need."

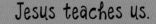

Jesus teaches us.

Jesus taught about prayer too. "Pray like this," He said. "Our Father in heaven, may your name be kept holy. May your Kingdom come soon. May your will be done on earth, as it is in heaven. Give us today the food we need, and forgive us our sins, as we have forgiven those who sin against us. And don't let us yield to temptation, but rescue us from the evil one" [Matthew 6:9–13 NLT].

Jesus had so many things to teach His followers! He gave them an important rule we call the golden rule: "Whatever you would like others to do for you, do that for them. This is how God wants you to live."

And Jesus reminded everyone that God is good. "Ask, seek, and knock," He said. "God is your good Father. He wants to give you good things, and He will!"

WHAT DOES IT MEAN?

Do you like to learn new things? What do you like learning about the most?

Many different people teach us many different things as we grow. Moms and dads help us learn to eat, walk, talk, ride a bike, and have good manners. Coaches teach us to swim, do gymnastics, and play soccer. Teachers at school help us learn our ABCs and numbers, to read and do math. Sunday school teachers help us learn about the Bible.

Jesus was often called *Teacher*. His students were His disciples. They listened to Jesus' words, and they watched what He did. That is how they learned to do the things that please God, and that is how we learn from Jesus too!

LEARN MORE

There were many teachers in Israel, but Jesus was the wisest and best. When He was only twelve years old, He amazed the temple teachers. You can read the story in Luke 2:41–52.

WHAT HAPPENED NEXT?

Before Jesus finished teaching His disciples on the mountainside, He told them an important story . . .

Dear God, thank You for Jesus, my Teacher.
I like learning from Him! Amen.

A Tale of Two Builders

The cornerstone is Christ Jesus himself.
—Ephesians 2:20 NLT

FROM MATTHEW 7; LUKE 6. Jesus looked at His disciples and out over the crowd. He had been talking to them for a long time, and they were still listening carefully to His words.

"I've taught you about many things today," He said. "I've spoken a lot of words, and they are important words. But you must *do* what the words say if you want to be wise. Don't just listen to the words and walk away."

Then Jesus told this story to help people remember to obey His words:

A wise man wanted to build a new house. Where should he build it? He wanted his house to last for many years. He wanted it to be a strong, safe house, even in the middle of a storm.

So the man found some land and dug down deep to the rocky layer underground. He laid the foundation for his house on the rock. Then he cut, and stacked, and sanded, and pounded until his house was done.

One day, the man saw dark clouds gathering in the sky. "Storm's coming!" he said. "I'd better get inside."

Thunder *crashed*! Lightning *flashed*! Rain poured down and caused a flood. Fierce winds beat against the man's house. Would the house survive the storm?

Yes! When the storm ended, the house that was built on the rock was still standing, good as new.

Another man also wanted to build a new house. But this foolish man built his house right on top of the shifting sand. When thunder *crashed*, lightning *flashed*, rain poured down and caused a flood, and fierce winds beat against *that* house, what happened? That house fell down because it was built on sand!

Jesus is the only strong foundation.

"Learn from this story," Jesus said. "If you hear My words and do them, you will be like the wise man who built his house on the rock, with a strong foundation. But if you hear My words and don't do what I say, you will be like the foolish man who built his house on the sand."

WHAT DOES IT MEAN?

Do you take lessons? Maybe you take piano lessons, swimming lessons, or dance lessons. Whenever we take lessons to learn something new, we learn basic skills first. They are the *foundation* to support the harder skills we learn later on.

Every house has a foundation—a beginning—usually made of concrete or concrete blocks. When the Bible was written, foundations were made of stone. An important part of any foundation was the cornerstone, the first and largest stone of the foundation. Without the cornerstone in place, a house would fall down.

Jesus is the *Cornerstone* because He is our strong foundation. If we listen to Jesus *and* do what He says, we will have good lives no matter what happens.

LEARN MORE

- First Corinthians 3:9–11 says, "You are a house that belongs to God. Like an expert builder I built the foundation of that house. . . . The foundation that has already been laid is Jesus Christ" (ICB).
- James 1:22, 25 says, "Do what God's teaching says; do not just listen and do nothing. . . . The truly happy person is the one who . . . listens to God's teaching and does not forget what he heard. Then he obeys what God's teaching says. When he does this, it makes him happy" (ICB).

WHAT HAPPENED NEXT?

Many people believed in Jesus. He had shown them His power by healing and teaching. But one day, Jesus showed His disciples that He truly was the Son of God . . .

Dear God, I want to listen to Jesus and do what He says. Please help me. I love You! Amen.

Trouble at Sea

They went and woke him, saying, "Master, Master, we are perishing!"
—Luke 8:24

FROM MATTHEW 8; MARK 4; LUKE 8. Sometimes Jesus stayed so busy teaching and healing people that He and His disciples didn't even have time to sleep. Jesus was glad to help people in these ways, but sometimes He needed to rest.

Near the end of one busy day, Jesus said to His disciples, "Let's go across to the other side of the lake." So they all got into a boat, and soon Jesus fell asleep on a cushion at the back of the boat.

After a while, a strong wind howled and churned up the waves on the lake. But Jesus didn't wake up.

"The waves are getting bigger!" the disciples said to one another. "Oh no! Hold on! Here comes a wave that's going to crash right on top of us!" The big wave rocked the boat on its side, and water began filling the boat. "We're going to sink if this keeps up!" the disciples yelled. "We might drown!"

But Jesus still didn't wake up.

Everywhere the disciples looked, giant waves were all they could see. The wind and the waves kept pounding the boat.

But through it all, Jesus didn't wake up.

Finally, some of the disciples went to the back of the boat, where Jesus was still sleeping. "Master, Master!" they cried. "Save us! Don't You care that we're going to drown?"

Jesus woke up. He saw the storm and His frightened friends. And He knew what to do. "Wind, that's enough!" He said.

The wind stopped blowing.

"Peace! Be still!" Jesus said to the sea.

The waves stopped crashing, and the water was calm.

Jesus turned to His disciples. "Why were you afraid? Where is your faith?"

The disciples didn't know how to answer Him. But they said to one another, "How amazing and wonderful Jesus is! Even the winds and the waves obey Him!"

Jesus rules over all.

WHAT DOES IT MEAN?

Do you like music? What is your favorite song? Have you ever heard an orchestra?

In an orchestra are many different kinds of musical instruments— violins, trombones, clarinets, drums, and lots more! Standing at the front of the orchestra is the conductor. All the musicians keep their eyes on the conductor and play their instruments the way he wants them to because the conductor is the master of the orchestra—he's the leader, and he's in charge.

One of Jesus' names in the Bible is *Master*. The disciples called Jesus that because He was their leader. But Jesus also is Master over the world. Everything about creation—even the weather—must obey Him. He's in charge.

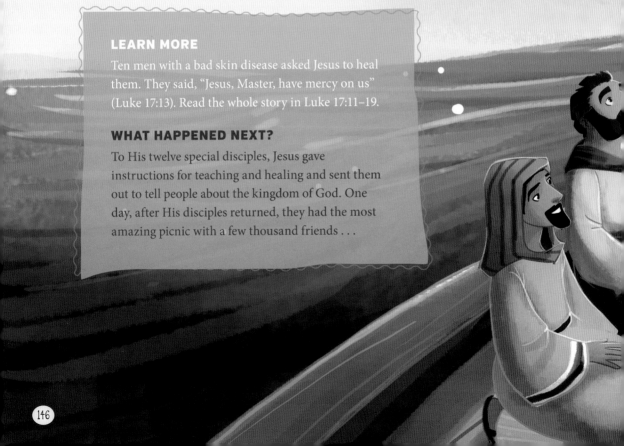

LEARN MORE

Ten men with a bad skin disease asked Jesus to heal them. They said, "Jesus, Master, have mercy on us" (Luke 17:13). Read the whole story in Luke 17:11–19.

WHAT HAPPENED NEXT?

To His twelve special disciples, Jesus gave instructions for teaching and healing and sent them out to tell people about the kingdom of God. One day, after His disciples returned, they had the most amazing picnic with a few thousand friends . . .

Dear God, thank You for such a good and powerful Master—Jesus! I'm glad He's in charge of the world. Amen.

Feeding Hungry People

"I am the bread that gives life. He who comes to me will never be hungry."
—John 6:35 ICB

FROM MATTHEW 14; MARK 6; LUKE 9; JOHN 6. "Jesus took a boat to Bethsaida!" people told one another. "If we hurry, we can see Him!" The road along the shore filled quickly. Healthy people ran. "Oops, sorry! Didn't mean to bump into you." Sick people walked or rode a donkey, or someone carried them.

Jesus saw the crowd coming. He smiled at people to welcome them. How much they needed Him! All day, He healed the sick and taught about God's kingdom.

But late in the afternoon, Jesus' disciples began to worry. "What are we going to do?" they asked Him. "We're out here in a lonely place, and all these people are hungry! We'd better send them away to buy food, or they won't have the strength to walk home."

"We don't need to do that," Jesus said. "You can feed them."

What did Jesus mean? "We don't have food for all these people!" the disciples said. "And we don't have enough money to buy food for everyone."

But Jesus wasn't worried. He knew what He was going to do. "What do you have?" He asked. "Does anyone here have any food at all? Go and see."

Jesus gives us life
that never ends.

The disciples scattered through the crowd. Andrew found a boy with a little lunch—five loaves of barley bread and two tiny dried fish. He brought the boy to Jesus.

"This young man has a small lunch," Andrew said. "But it's not enough to feed thousands of people!"

"Tell everyone to sit down in groups," Jesus said.

When everyone was settled, Jesus looked up to heaven and thanked God for the food. Then He broke the loaves and fish into pieces for His disciples to take to the crowd.

In their groups, people passed the bread and fish to one another.

"Mmm, this tastes heavenly!" they said. "And there is so much! Would you like another piece?" Little children held bread and fish in each hand and laughed and smiled as they ate.

The five little loaves and two small fish didn't run out until everyone felt full and no one wanted another bite!

"Let's not waste anything," Jesus said. "Gather up the leftovers." The disciples filled twelve big baskets with fish and bread.

"Amazing!" the people said. "Our ancestors ate manna, and we ate this fish and bread! Jesus must be the One we have been waiting for!"

The next day, Jesus talked about what He had done. "I am the Bread of Life," He said. "Listen to me and believe. Then you will live and never be hungry."

WHAT DOES IT MEAN?

How do you like to eat bread? Do you like it toasted for breakfast, or with peanut butter and jelly for lunch? How about warm rolls or corn bread with butter and honey at dinnertime? Bread tastes good, it fills us up, and it gives our bodies energy and nutrition. People all over the world eat bread.

Jesus said He is the *Bread of Life*. Just as our bodies need food so we can live and grow, we need Jesus so we can live with God in heaven someday. Even after a good meal, we will get hungry again. But when we believe in Jesus and He fills us up with His words and His presence, we have life right now *and* later on in heaven too!

Dear God, thank You for Jesus, the Bread of Life. Help me be filled up with His words and His presence today and every day. Amen.

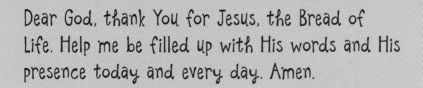

LEARN MORE

Jesus said, "I am the way, and the truth, and the life" (John 14:6).

WHAT HAPPENED NEXT?

Some of the people wanted to make Jesus their king. But Jesus knew that was not part of God's plan, so He walked away. But then He took another walk that wasn't just on land . . .

I AM

Jehovah (jeh-HO-vah)

Walking on Water

He spoke to them, saying, Take courage! I AM! Stop being afraid!
—Matthew 14:27 AMP

FROM MATTHEW 14; MARK 6; JOHN 6. Soon it would be night. "Go back to the boat now," Jesus told His disciples, "and head back across the lake. I'll say good-bye to all the people here." After the disciples rowed away and Jesus sent the crowd home, He climbed up the mountainside by Himself to pray.

When it was dark, Jesus was still praying. The disciples were a long way from land, but Jesus could see they were having trouble. A strong wind blew against the boat and made it hard for them to row.

Jesus prayed a little while longer. Then He climbed down the mountain and went to join His disciples. But Jesus didn't go in a boat—He walked on the water!

The disciples saw Jesus coming toward them, but they didn't know it was Him. "Look! A ghost!" they cried out.

"Have courage!" Jesus called to them. "I am with you! Don't be afraid!"

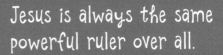

Peter, one of the disciples, said, "Lord, if it is You, tell me to walk to You on the water."

Jesus smiled. "Come on then, Peter!" He said.

Peter climbed up on the side of the boat. Then he climbed down and stepped onto the water. Would he sink? No! Peter kept his eyes on Jesus and started walking toward Him on the water! One step, two steps, three steps, four steps . . .

But then Peter looked away from Jesus and looked at all the waves instead—and he felt afraid and began to sink. "Lord, save me!" he cried.

Jesus reached out His hand and pulled Peter up. "Oh, Peter," He said. "Your faith is small. Why did you doubt?" Together they got into the boat.

Dear God, thank You that Jesus is always the same and always powerful. I love You, and I love Jesus! Amen.

And when they did, the wind stopped blowing, and suddenly the boat was at the shore.

Peter and all the disciples worshiped Jesus right there in the boat. "You *are* the Son of God!" they said.

WHAT DOES IT MEAN?

Have you learned how to swim? At the beach or a swimming pool, it's important to have a swimming buddy, to stay where grown-ups can see you, and to follow other safety rules. People can learn to swim, and some people can learn to do special dives with somersaults and twists. But when it comes to walking, people were made to walk on dry ground, not on water.

So how could Jesus walk on water? Because Jesus is God. Do you remember reading about Moses and the burning bush? God talked to Moses from the bush. When Moses asked God His name, God said, "I AM." When Jesus walked on the water toward the disciples, He told them the same thing. He said, "*I AM.* Don't be afraid." Jesus had power to walk on water, and He had power to let Peter do it too.

Jesus, *I AM*, is always the same powerful ruler over all. We can trust and worship Him!

LEARN MORE

Many people didn't believe that Jesus was God's Son. But Jesus said to them, "I tell you the truth, before Abraham was even born, I AM!" (John 8:58 NLT).

WHAT HAPPENED NEXT?

Some people thought Jesus would free the Jews from the Romans who ruled over them. But Jesus knew that was not why He had come. There was a more important reason . . .

The Most Important Thing

In the beginning was the Word, and the Word was with God, and the Word was God.
—John 1:1

FROM LUKE 10. In the village of Bethany lived two sisters—Mary and Martha—and their brother, Lazarus.

Martha saw Jesus walking through the village with His disciples. "Please come to our home and visit with us," Martha said. And Jesus agreed.

"Welcome, Jesus!" Martha said when Jesus arrived. "Come in and sit for a while."

Jesus made Himself comfortable in the living room. Martha ran to the kitchen to begin making dinner, but Mary came in and sat on the floor near Jesus. Oh, how she loved hearing Jesus teach about God! She listened to every word He said.

In the kitchen, Martha heated the oven. She chopped vegetables. She stirred a sauce for the meat. She mixed flour and oil for bread, and she rolled and kneaded the dough until it was ready to bake. This dinner was important! Everything had to be just right for Jesus! Would everything be ready on time? Martha was getting worried. Where was her sister, Mary, and why wasn't Mary helping her?

Jesus speaks to us.

Martha wiped her hands on a towel and went to look for Mary.

She wasn't outside. She wasn't doing laundry. She wasn't taking a nap.

Oh, there she was! Mary was sitting on the floor, not doing anything, just listening to Jesus.

Humph! Martha thought. *I'll ask Jesus what He thinks about that!*

Martha stomped into the living room. "Jesus!" she said. "I have a lot of cooking and serving to do! Don't you care that my sister isn't working with me in the kitchen? Tell her to come and help me!"

Jesus looked at Martha and smiled. "Martha, Martha," He said. "You're so worried and upset about many things. But only one thing is necessary, and that is what Mary has chosen. She's chosen the good thing—listening to Me. And that will never be taken away from her."

WHAT DOES IT MEAN?

Words, words, words! Words are everywhere. Most grown-ups speak sixteen thousand words every day! We talk to our friends. We hear words on TV. We hear words on the radio. We read words in books and on apps.

Some words are *very* important to say and to hear, words like "I love you," "Can I help you?" and "I'm sorry." But the most important words of all are God's words.

When Mary listened to Jesus, she was listening to God's words. We listen to Jesus, *The Word*, when we read the Bible. Listening to Jesus is the most important thing we'll ever do!

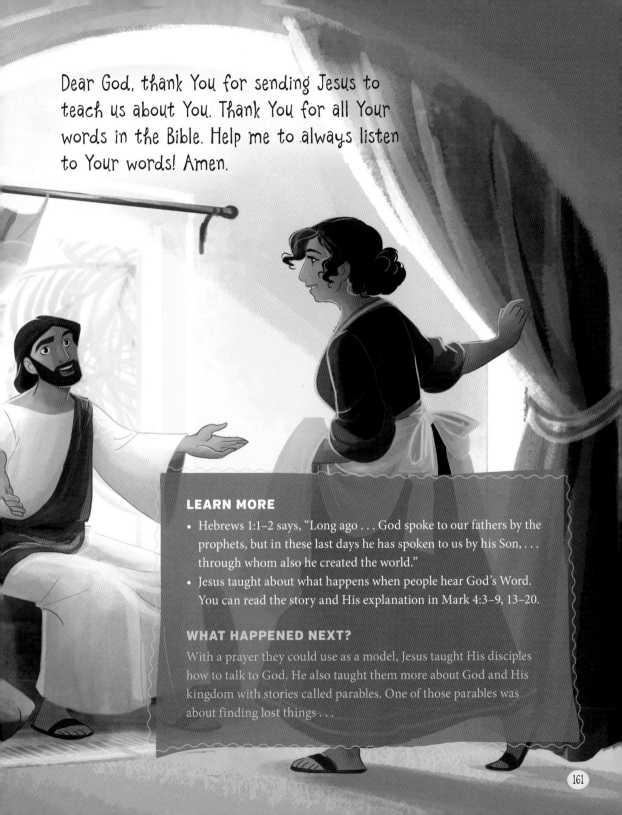

Dear God, thank You for sending Jesus to teach us about You. Thank You for all Your words in the Bible. Help me to always listen to Your words! Amen.

LEARN MORE

- Hebrews 1:1–2 says, "Long ago . . . God spoke to our fathers by the prophets, but in these last days he has spoken to us by his Son, . . . through whom also he created the world."
- Jesus taught about what happens when people hear God's Word. You can read the story and His explanation in Mark 4:3–9, 13–20.

WHAT HAPPENED NEXT?

With a prayer they could use as a model, Jesus taught His disciples how to talk to God. He also taught them more about God and His kingdom with stories called parables. One of those parables was about finding lost things . . .

Finding the Lost Sheep

"I am the good shepherd. The good shepherd lays down his life for the sheep."
—John 10:11

FROM MATTHEW 18; LUKE 15. People of all kinds came to hear Jesus teach about God.

People who thought they weren't as good as other people came. They were surprised that Jesus was happy to see them and that He often sat down to eat with them.

People who had always loved God came.

And people who thought they were better than others came. They grumbled about Jesus eating with the people they called sinners. So Jesus told them a story about a shepherd who had one hundred sheep.

A shepherd watched over his sheep carefully every day and every night. To make sure that none of the sheep wandered away from the rest of the flock, he counted them. One sheep, two sheep, three sheep, four sheep . . . all the way to one hundred. But one day when the shepherd counted his sheep, he had only ninety-nine. One sheep was missing! One sheep had wandered off and might be in trouble!

Jesus searches for people who are far from God.

The shepherd wanted to find his lost sheep right away. So he left his flock in a safe place on the mountain, and he began to search for the one sheep that had wandered away.

He searched everywhere, up hills and down. Under bushes. Behind trees. Down in the creeks. Up on the cliffs. He listened carefully, and finally he heard a faint *baa-baa-baa-ing*.

Yes! There was the lost sheep, caught in a bramble bush, worn out, hurt, and hungry. The shepherd picked up the sheep and put it around his shoulders. Then he started his journey home.

When he got back to his flock, he cared for the sheep that had been lost, giving him food and water and a good place to rest. Then he called to his friends and neighbors, "Hurrah! Be happy for me! I've found my lost sheep!"

When His story ended, Jesus said, "Remember, God is like that shepherd. He rejoices over those who are always at His side, but He celebrates even more when someone lost is found."

WHAT DOES IT MEAN?

Have you ever lost something important to you? What was it? You probably looked *everywhere* for what you lost—under your bed, in your closet, on your toy shelves, maybe even in the trash! Or maybe you have a pet that got lost, and you walked all over your neighborhood with your mom or dad, looking for your lost pet. Did you find what had been lost? What did you do then? How did you feel?

A good shepherd goes looking for every lost sheep and is so happy when he finds it. Jesus said He is the *Good Shepherd*. He came to earth from heaven to look for lost people—people who had wandered far from God. And whenever someone far from God believes in Jesus—God and all heaven rejoice!

Dear God, I'm glad I have a good shepherd like Jesus to care for me and keep me safe! Amen.

LEARN MORE

"My sheep hear my voice, and I know them, and they follow me" (John 10:27).

WHAT HAPPENED NEXT?

Sometimes people stop listening to God and obeying Him. How do you think God feels about them when they realize they are wrong? Jesus told a story that shows exactly how God feels when that happens . . .

A Good Father

You, O LORD, are our Father.
—Isaiah 63:16

FROM LUKE 15. Jesus told this story about a father who loved his sons just as God loves us:

A father owned a house and fields and had two grown sons. Someday each of the sons would receive a share of the land, but the younger son didn't want to wait. "Give me my share now," he said to his father. The father was sad, but he agreed.

Then the younger son sold his land and took his money and left. He went to another country, far away. He wasted all his money, and soon it was gone. Now what would he do? He was getting hungry, and he needed money to buy food. He got a job feeding pigs.

"Here, piggies!" he called. "Supper time!" The son was so hungry that he wished he could eat the pigs' food too. But no one gave him anything to eat.

One day, the son sat down to think. "My father's hired servants have plenty to eat," he said. "I will go back to my father. I will say, 'Father, I have sinned against God and against you. I'm not worthy to be called your son anymore. But please take me back as one of your hired servants.'" So he got up and began the trip home.

God gives good gifts to His children.

His father was waiting for him. Every day, his father had been watching for him!

The father saw his son while he was still far off. He felt compassion for his son and ran to meet him! The father hugged and kissed him.

"Father, I'm not good enough to be your son anymore," the son said.

But the father called to his servants and said, "Quick! Bring the best robe. Put a ring on his hand and sandals on his feet. And fix a great feast. It's time for a party—because my son, who was lost, is alive again. He has come home!"

The older son, working out in his father's fields, heard the sounds of the party. "What's going on?" he asked.

"Your brother has come home!" the servants told him.

Instead of being happy about this, the older son felt angry and jealous. "All this work I've done for you," he said to his father, "and you have never thrown a party for me! But my brother wasted your money, and now you are having a party for him!"

"Son, you have always been with me," the father said, "and everything I have is yours. We have to celebrate and be glad now because your brother was lost, but now he is found."

Dear God, I'm so glad You are my heavenly Father! Thank You for all the ways You are a good Father to me! Amen.

WHAT DOES IT MEAN?

Have you ever fallen asleep in the car at night, maybe on the way home from visiting your grandparents or your cousins? It's past your bedtime when you get home, and your dad scoops you up out of your seat. You can feel his strong arms as he carries you to your bedroom and tucks you into bed. You wake up just enough to smile and say good night.

One of God's names is *Father*. We have fathers on earth, but God is our Father in heaven. Even before the world began, God planned to send Jesus to die for our sins so God could forgive us, adopt us as His children, and be our Father.

God is a good Father. He cares for us and gives us good gifts—the beautiful world we live in, the people we love, and so much more! God carries us through every day, just as your dad carries you into bed from the car. "The everlasting God is your place of safety. His arms will hold you up forever" (Deuteronomy 33:27 ICB).

LEARN MORE
- Jesus taught His disciples to pray to God as their Father in heaven (Matthew 6:9).
- Jesus said, "I and the Father are one" (John 10:30).

WHAT HAPPENED NEXT?

Jesus got a message that His friend Lazarus was very sick. But rather than going to see Lazarus right away to make him well, Jesus stayed where He was for two more days. What was He waiting for? . . .

Lazarus Lives Again

Jesus said to her, "I am the resurrection and the life."
—John 11:25 ICB

FROM JOHN 10–11. "What are we going to do about Jesus?" asked the angry teachers and leaders in Jerusalem. They were jealous of Jesus because the people loved Him so much. And they thought it was wrong for Jesus to say He was God's Son. They refused to believe that He really was!

The teachers and leaders wanted to arrest Him, but Jesus slipped away and went to stay in a remote place near the Jordan River. While He was there, someone from Bethany, a village near Jerusalem, brought Him a message from Mary and Martha: "Our brother, Lazarus, the friend You love, is very sick."

Jesus did love Lazarus and his sisters. They were His friends. Jesus knew Mary and Martha wanted Him to come and heal Lazarus right away, but He didn't go. He stayed right where He was for two more days. Then He said to His disciples, "It's time for us to go back."

"But Jesus, the teachers and leaders in Jerusalem still want to arrest You," the disciples said. "Bethany is close to Jerusalem. It's dangerous to go back."

"Our friend Lazarus is dead," Jesus said. "Let's go to Bethany."

When Mary and Martha heard that Jesus was coming, Martha hurried to meet Him on the road. "Lord, if You had been here, my brother would not have died!" she said.

"Your brother will rise again," Jesus told her.

Jesus has power over life and death.

When Mary saw Jesus, she said, "Lord, if You had been here, my brother would not have died!" Mary was crying, and so were the friends who were with her. Jesus cried too because they were so sad.

"Where is Lazarus?" He asked.

"Come and see," they told him. They led Him to the tomb, a place like a cave, covered with a large stone.

"Take away the stone," Jesus said.

"Oh no! We can't do that!" Martha said.

"Didn't I tell you," Jesus said kindly, "that if you believe, you will see God's glory?"

So the stone was rolled away. Then Jesus prayed, "Father, let the people here believe that You sent Me," and He called in a loud voice, "Lazarus, come out!"

No one moved. No one even whispered. What was going to happen? Suddenly, everyone saw Lazarus standing near the front of the tomb! The man who had been dead was alive! His hands and feet were wrapped with linen strips, and a linen cloth was on his head.

"Unwrap him," Jesus said, "and let him go."

WHAT DOES IT MEAN?

Have you ever seen a tree with beautiful red, gold, and orange leaves? In some places, when summer is over and autumn comes, the leaves of some kinds of trees change color. We enjoy their beauty until, after a while, the leaves die and fall off the tree. The tree trunk and branches are bare. The tree looks dead. But when spring comes and the weather gets warmer, new leaves begin to bud and grow! The tree has new life!

Jesus told Martha, "I am *The Resurrection and the Life.*" When we believe in Jesus, we have new life that lasts forever. Even if our bodies die, we still live in heaven. Jesus has power over life and death!

LEARN MORE

John 6:40 says, "This is the will of my Father, that everyone who looks on the Son and believes in him should have eternal life, and I will raise him up on the last day."

WHAT HAPPENED NEXT?

Jesus returned to Jerusalem with His disciples, even though there was danger. He knew that was what God wanted Him to do . . .

Dear God, I'm glad You have power over everything. And I'm glad that someday I can live in heaven with You. Amen.

Parade for a King

He first found his own brother Simon and said to him, "We have found the Messiah" (which means Christ).
—John 1:41

FROM MATTHEW 21; MARK 11; LUKE 19; JOHN 12. Jesus and His disciples walked toward Jerusalem near the time of the Passover Feast. But as they got closer, Jesus told two of the disciples, "Go into the village nearby, and you will find a donkey colt no one has ever ridden. Untie the colt and bring it here. If anyone asks you what you are doing, say, 'The Lord has need of it, and He will send it back to you soon,' and they will let you bring the colt here."

So the disciples did what Jesus said. They found the young donkey and untied it. "Why are you untying the colt?" the owners asked.

"The Lord has need of it," the disciples said, "and He will send it back to you soon."

"All right then," the owners said. So the disciples led the colt to Jesus.

On the Mount of Olives, where Jesus was waiting for them, some of the disciples put their coats on the young donkey to make a place for Jesus to sit. Then they all started out for Jerusalem again, with Jesus riding the donkey and His disciples walking beside and behind Him.

People from the villages came and joined the parade. Some put their coats on the road to make a colorful pathway for Jesus to ride on. Others cut down palm branches to lay on the road. "Praise God!" people shouted. "He has done great things! Blessed is the King who comes in His name, the One He has sent!"

People had come to Jerusalem from far away to celebrate the Passover Feast. They had heard about Jesus and all the wonderful things He had done. "Hurrah!" they said to one another. "Jesus is coming! He's riding into the city on a donkey! Let's go see our King!"

They hurried out of the city to meet Jesus and join the parade. Along the way, they cut down big, leafy branches from the palm trees to wave as Jesus passed by. "Hosanna!" they shouted. "Blessed is He who comes in the name of the Lord!"

Jesus is the One God sent.

181

WHAT DOES IT MEAN?

On your birthday or on holidays, do you ever get mail? Who sends you mail? What kind of mail do you get? It's fun to open letters, cards, and gifts someone has sent to us!

Do you remember that after Adam and Eve disobeyed God in the garden of Eden, God promised that someday He would send Someone to make things right again? That Someone was Jesus! One of Jesus' names in the Bible is *Christ*, which means "anointed one." God *anointed* — or chose — His Son, Jesus, to come to earth to die for our sins and to be the ruler of God's people. And when the right time came, God did what He said He would do — He sent Jesus, the greatest gift ever given!

Dear God, thank You for Your promise to send Someone to lead Your people and to make things right again. Thank You for sending Jesus! Amen.

Serve One Another

"Here is my servant . . . the one I chose."
—Isaiah 42:1 ICB

FROM MATTHEW 26; MARK 14; LUKE 22; JOHN 13. "It's nearly time for the Passover Feast," Jesus told two of His disciples. "Go into the city. You will see a man carrying a water jar. Follow him to a house, and say to the owner of the house, 'The Teacher needs to eat the Passover meal here.' The owner of the house will show you an upstairs room. You can get the food ready for us to eat together there."

The disciples did what Jesus said. They found the house and the Upper Room, and they talked to the owner of the house. Then they got everything ready for the feast.

Jesus and the other disciples arrived at supper time. "I'm glad I can celebrate Passover with all of you tonight," Jesus said. "I've been looking forward to this very much!"

During the meal, Jesus held up some bread and a cup from the table. "This bread is like My body," He said, "and this drink is like My blood. I will be giving them for you. Remember Me whenever you eat this bread and drink this cup." Jesus was telling His disciples that soon He was going to die for the sins of the world—but they didn't understand.

Then, after supper, Jesus had one more important lesson for His disciples.

He got up from the table and took off His robe. He poured water into a big bowl and tied a towel around His waist.

What was Jesus doing? The disciples didn't know.

Then Jesus knelt in front of the disciples one by one and washed their feet!

Usually a servant did a dusty, dirty job like washing the feet of dinner guests!

Jesus served others and shows us how to serve others too.

"Jesus, what are You doing?" Peter asked.

Jesus finished His work. Then He said, "You all call Me your Lord and your Teacher, and those names are true. So if your Lord and Teacher has washed your feet like a servant, then you also must serve one another. When I washed your feet tonight, I gave you an example to follow. And you will be blessed if you do this."

WHAT DOES IT MEAN?

In Bible times, walking in sandals on dusty roads gave people dirty feet. Some families had servants to cook and serve meals, and those same servants often washed the feet of guests who came to dinner.

One of Jesus' names in the Bible is *Servant*. A good servant does what is good for others. Kings often had many servants. Jesus, God's Son, is the King of kings, but instead of people serving Him, Jesus served people! He left His beautiful home in heaven and came to live with people on earth. He taught about God, and He healed the sick. Then He gave His life for the sins of the world so the people who love Him can live with God in heaven forever.

Dear God, I want to do what Jesus said. I want to serve others like He did. Please show me how I can be a good helper. Amen.

LEARN MORE

A Roman soldier with many servants came to Jesus for help. You can read the story in Luke 7:2–10.

WHAT HAPPENED NEXT?

Jesus and His disciples went out to a garden, where Jesus prayed. Then temple leaders, who did not like Jesus, sent soldiers to arrest Him. Jesus could have stopped them with just a word, but He did not. He knew what was happening was part of God's plan to save His people . . .

From Sad to Glad

Grace and peace from God the Father and Christ Jesus our Savior.
—Titus 1:4

FROM MATTHEW 26–28; MARK 14–16; LUKE 22–24; JOHN 18–20.
When Jesus was arrested in the garden, the disciples were afraid. Why was Jesus letting this happen? Why didn't He stop the soldiers from taking Him away? The disciples didn't understand this was all part of God's plan, and they all ran away.

Peter followed Jesus and the soldiers to the home of the high priest, where the temple leaders had gathered. But Peter was afraid the soldiers might arrest him too, and so three times he told the people around him, "I don't know Jesus."

Then the temple leaders sent Jesus to the Roman ruler. Pilate knew Jesus hadn't done anything wrong. But he was afraid of the angry crowd, which was getting bigger and louder, so he let the temple leaders have their way. Jesus would die on a cross.

What a sad day! And Jesus could have stopped it all, but He didn't. He trusted His Father and did what God wanted Him to do.

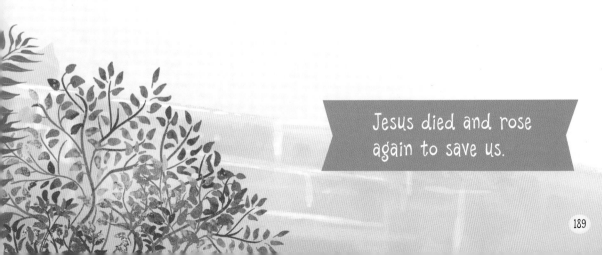

Jesus died and rose again to save us.

The soldiers led Jesus out to a lonely place, where they nailed His hands and feet to a big wooden cross. "It is finished!" Jesus said, and then He died.

Late in the day, a man named Joseph asked for permission to take Jesus' body down from the cross. Joseph laid Jesus' body in a tomb cut into the rock and rolled a big stone across the front.

On the third day, early in the morning, several women set out to go to the tomb. They wanted to put sweet-smelling perfumes and spices on Jesus' body. "But who will roll the stone away for us?" they asked each other.

At the tomb, the women stopped, surprised. "Look! The stone has already been rolled away! How did that happen?" They didn't know an angel had done it.

Slowly, they stepped into the tomb—and saw two angels in shining white robes!

"Don't be afraid!" the angels said. "You are looking for Jesus, but He is not here. He has risen, just as He told you He would! See the place where they laid Him. Now go and tell His disciples and Peter that He is going to Galilee, and you will see Him there."

Could it be true? The women didn't know what to say. They turned around and hurried to find the disciples to give them the angels' message.

But one of the women went back. She was crying. And then something amazing happened— she saw Jesus, and He talked with her!

Oh, what a happy day! Jesus was alive again. He had risen, just as He said!

Dear God, thank You for Jesus, the Savior! Thank You for wanting to save us so we can live with You forever. Amen.

WHAT DOES IT MEAN?

When there's a problem, but someone does something to fix that problem, we say that person "saved the day." When a basketball team is about to lose a game, for example, but one of the players suddenly scores and her team wins instead of losing, we say that player saved the day for her team.

One of the names for Jesus in the Bible is *Savior*. A savior "saves the day"—fixes a problem—for someone else. Our sins are a problem. When Jesus died on the cross for our sins and rose again, He "saved the day" for us. If we believe in Him, we can live with God in heaven forever!

LEARN MORE

First John 4:14 says, "We have seen with our own eyes . . . that the Father sent his Son to be the Savior of the world" (NLT).

WHAT HAPPENED NEXT?

For forty days before He went back to heaven, Jesus appeared at different times and in different places, encouraging His followers to believe in Him. Some people believed simply because they *heard* that Jesus was alive again, but one disciple needed more proof . . .

Could It Be True?

The free gift of God is eternal life in Christ Jesus our Lord.
—Romans 6:23

FROM MARK 16; LUKE 24; JOHN 20. After Jesus died, His disciples stayed together in one place, and they kept the door locked. They were afraid of the leaders and rulers who had arrested Jesus and killed Him on the cross. They didn't want anything else bad to happen.

And then they heard good news from the women who had gone to Jesus' tomb. The women said Jesus was alive! His body was not in the tomb! An angel had told them that Jesus had risen, and Mary had even said that she'd seen Him! Could it all really be true?

Oh, how the disciples wanted it to be true! But they weren't sure . . .

And then that evening, while they were together in an upper room, with the door locked, suddenly—Jesus was standing right there too! Could it really be Him—or was this a ghost? The disciples didn't know what to think or what to do. They were afraid.

Jesus wants us to believe in Him,
trust Him, and obey Him.

"Be at peace," Jesus told them. "There's no need to be troubled. You don't need to doubt. It's really Me—see My hands and My feet." He showed the disciples the places in His hands and feet where the nails had been. "You can touch Me," He said. "I have a body."

Oh, this was wonderful! Jesus was alive!

"Do you have anything to eat?" Jesus asked. They gave Him some fish, and He ate it while they watched. Yes, this really *was* Jesus. How amazing and wonderful! The glad news they had heard was *true*!

But one of the disciples, Thomas, wasn't with the others when Jesus came to see them. "Thomas, Thomas! It's true, it's true!" the disciples told Thomas when he came back. "Jesus is alive!" they said. "We have seen Him! We saw the places in His hands and feet where the nails were."

Thomas shook his head. "I just don't believe it," he said. "And I won't believe it unless I can put my hands on the places where the nails were."

The next time the disciples were all together, eight days later, Thomas was there. And suddenly, Jesus was there too!

"Thomas, put your hands here, where the nails were," Jesus said. "See that it is really Me, and believe."

Thomas saw and touched Jesus' hands where the nails had been. "My Lord and my God!"

"Now you believe because you have seen Me" Jesus said. "That is good. But blessed are those who haven't seen Me but still believe."

Dear God, I'm so glad to know that Jesus is alive! I believe, and I want to follow Him. Amen.

WHAT DOES IT MEAN?

In some places, children learn to say, "Yes, sir" and "No, sir," "Yes, ma'am" and "No ma'am" as a way of speaking politely to grown-ups. In Bible times, people often called men "my lord" to show them respect and be polite. But when Thomas called Jesus *Lord*, he was not just being polite. Thomas called Jesus *Lord* because he understood that Jesus is God's Son, the ruler over all!

LEARN MORE

First Corinthians 15:57 says, "We thank God! He gives us the victory through our Lord Jesus Christ" (ICB).

WHAT HAPPENED NEXT?

Many people saw Jesus alive at different times after the resurrection. But there was one disciple that Jesus especially wanted to see. Jesus had an important message just for him . . .

Breakfast with Jesus

"You are my friends if you do what I command you."
—John 15:14 ICB

FROM JOHN 21. Jesus was alive again—the disciples had seen Him with their own eyes! But where was He now? When would they see Him again? And what were they supposed to do in the meantime?

"I'm going fishing," Peter said.

"We'll go with you," said Thomas, Nathanael, James, John, and two other disciples.

They climbed into their fishing boat and rowed out on the lake. They threw their fishing nets into the water—*kersplash!* Then they waited . . . and waited . . . and waited. They waited all night. But they didn't catch any fish. Not one.

Jesus is our friend.

Just as morning came, Peter and the others saw a man standing on the shore, but they didn't know who it was.

The man called to them, "Friends, do you have any fish?"

"No," they answered. "Not one."

"Throw your net over the right side of the boat," the man said, "and you will find some."

"I guess we could try it," the disciples said to one another. They threw the big, heavy net into the water on the right side of the boat.

Suddenly, the net filled with fish — lots and lots of fish!

Something like this happened once before . . . , Peter, James, and John remembered.

"That man on the shore is the Lord!" John said.

Peter was so glad to see Jesus again that he jumped into the water and swam to shore while the other disciples brought in the boat. There on the beach, Peter saw Jesus and a little fire. Bread and fish were warming over the fire.

"Bring some of the fish you caught," Jesus said, "and let's have breakfast."

So Peter pulled the net full of fish onto the beach and brought some of the fish to Jesus.

When breakfast was ready, everyone gathered around the fire, and Jesus served the bread and fish to His friends.

Oh, how good it was for the disciples to be with Jesus again! Then Peter heard Jesus ask, "Peter, do you love Me more than these?"

"You know that I do, Lord," Peter said.

"Peter, do you love Me?" Jesus asked again.

"You know that I do, Lord," Peter said.

"Peter, do you love Me?" Jesus asked again.

That made three times Jesus had asked Peter the same question—just as Peter had denied knowing Jesus three times at the high priest's house. "Lord, You know everything!" Peter said. "You know that I love You."

"Feed My sheep," Jesus said, "and follow Me."

Jesus had forgiven Peter and given him important work to do!

WHAT DOES IT MEAN?

Who are some of your friends? What do you like to do with your friends? What do you think makes a good friend?

Jesus told His disciples, "Now I call you friends" (John 15:15 ICB). Friends know each other well. They like to do things together. Friends care about each other and help each other. Friends forgive. That's the kind of friend Jesus is!

Jesus is our *Friend* when we obey His commands— when we do what He says (John 15:14). He's the best friend we will ever have!

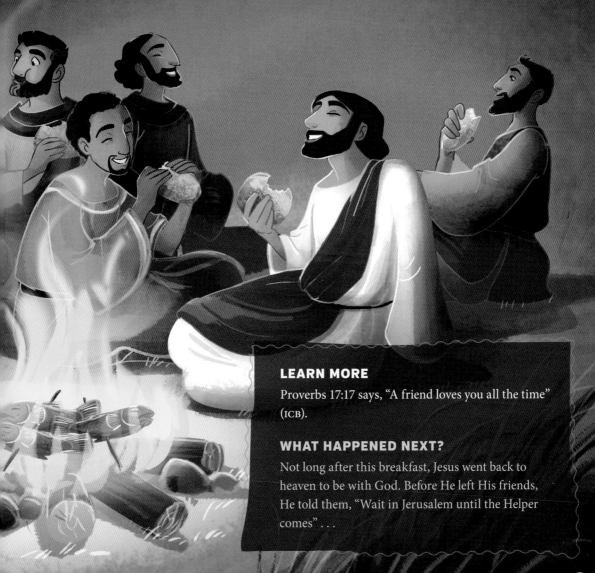

Dear God, thank You for Jesus, my very best friend. I love Him! Amen.

LEARN MORE

Proverbs 17:17 says, "A friend loves you all the time" (ICB).

WHAT HAPPENED NEXT?

Not long after this breakfast, Jesus went back to heaven to be with God. Before He left His friends, He told them, "Wait in Jerusalem until the Helper comes" . . .

The Church Begins

"I will ask the Father, and he will give you another Helper, to be with you forever."
—John 14:16

FROM LUKE 24; ACTS 1–2. Jesus led His disciples out of the city and up the Mount of Olives. It was time for Him to go back to heaven. "Remember, the Helper is coming," Jesus told the disciples. "Stay in Jerusalem until the Helper comes."

The disciples watched as Jesus went up into heaven. They worshiped Him and then went back to the city. "We will wait in Jerusalem as Jesus told us to do," they said, "until the promised Helper comes." So with Jesus' mother and brothers, the disciples prayed and waited in an upper room.

On the day of Pentecost, suddenly the sound of a loud, rushing wind filled the house where they all were. And then they saw what looked like tongues of fire resting on each person. The Helper—the Holy Spirit—had come!

The Holy Spirit helps us and gives us power.

The Holy Spirit filled each person, and everyone began to talk in different languages—languages they didn't know and had never learned to speak! All the disciples talking at the same time made a very loud sound.

Jerusalem had many visitors who had come from many lands for the feast of Pentecost. These people heard the noise coming from the upper room. "What's going on?" they wanted to know. "Let's go find out what's happening!" So they hurried to the street where the Upper Room was.

"Amazing!" said people from Asia and Egypt and Rome and Arabia. "These men who are talking are all from Galilee, but we hear them speaking

in our own languages, and we can understand them. They are talking about the mighty works of God!" The people listening to the disciples wondered why this was happening. "What does it mean?" they wanted to know.

Peter looked out at the crowd. He had never talked to that many people before! But now, with the Holy Spirit helping him, Peter spoke to them. He told the crowd how Jesus had died and that He rose again. "Jesus is the One God sent!" Peter said. "Jesus is Lord!"

Many in the crowd believed Peter's words. "What should we do?" they asked.

"Turn away from sinning, and be baptized," Peter told them. "You will receive the Holy Spirit too."

About three thousand new believers were added to the church that day!

WHAT DOES IT MEAN?

Have you ever fallen off your bike or your skateboard and hurt yourself? Who came to pick you up and take care of you? Who helps you learn new things at school? Who helps you at home when homework is hard? Who helps you when you are sick? We all need many kinds of help, and many people help us.

Jesus knew that when He went back to heaven, His followers would need a lot of help, and God sent the *Helper*, the Holy Spirit, to help us in many ways. The Helper gives us power to tell others about Jesus and to obey His commands. He gives us joy when we are sad. He lets us know we are not alone. He helps us pray when we don't know what to say, and He reminds us that God loves us very much!

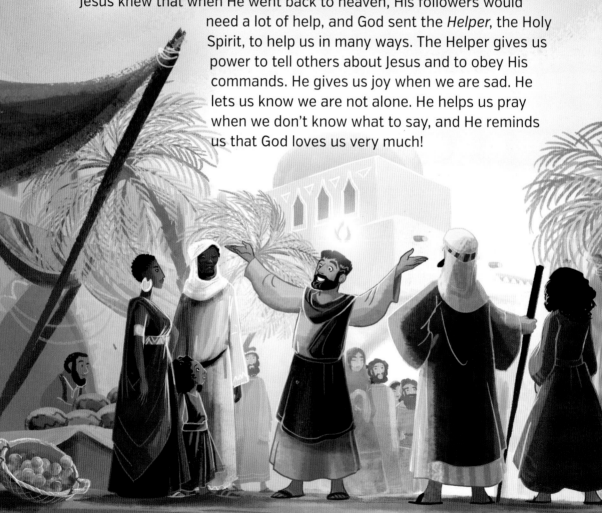

Dear God, thank You for all the ways You help me.
Thank You for the Holy Spirit. Amen.

LEARN MORE

Romans 8:26 says, "The Spirit helps us."

WHAT HAPPENED NEXT?

The news about Jesus spread throughout Jerusalem and beyond, and the church began to grow. But not everyone was happy about it. Some people, like Saul of Tarsus, made trouble for many new believers . . .

On the Damascus Road

"I am the light of the world."
—John 8:12

FROM ACTS 8–9. A man named Saul loved God and tried to obey Him always. In fact, Saul thought that obeying God's old laws was the way to get to heaven

someday. He didn't understand that God sent Jesus to give us new laws: to love God and to love one another. He didn't understand that Jesus died for the sins of everyone who would believe in Him. And He didn't understand that God saves us when we have faith in Him. Instead, Saul tried to stop people from believing in Jesus. He even put some of them in prison.

One day Saul began a trip to the city of Damascus. He planned to look for Christians there and bring them back to Jerusalem to put them in prison.

But on the road to Damascus, God changed Saul's plans.

"There's the city!" Saul said to his friends. "We're almost there."

Suddenly, Saul saw a brilliant light shining all around—so bright he couldn't look at it—and he fell down to the ground. Then Saul heard a voice say, "Saul, Saul, why are you hurting Me?"

"Who are You, Lord?" Saul asked.

Saul's friends heard the voice too, but they didn't know what was happening. Who was Saul talking to?

Jesus gives us His light so we can shine for Him.

"I am Jesus," the voice said, "and you are hurting Me when you hurt people who believe in Me. Go into the city now, and someone there will tell you what to do next."

Saul got up, but he couldn't see anything—he was blind! His friends led him by the hand into the city, and Saul stayed at the home of a man named Judas. For three days, he refused to eat or drink anything.

Then Jesus told a man named Ananias to visit Saul and heal him so Saul could see again. Ananias didn't want to go. "Are You sure, Lord?" Ananias asked. "I've heard about how mean Saul is!"

"Yes, go," Jesus said. "I've chosen Saul to do special work for Me. He will tell Gentiles and kings and the Jewish people about Me."

So Ananias went to visit Saul. "Brother Saul," he said, "you saw the Lord Jesus on the road to Damascus, and now He has sent me here so you can see again and be filled with the Holy Spirit."

Right away, something like fish scales fell from Saul's eyes. "I can see again!" Saul said. He got up and was baptized, and then he had something to eat.

Now Saul knew that the way to be saved is to know Jesus, God's Son, and he wanted to tell everyone he could. So that is just what he did!

WHAT DOES IT MEAN?

Have you ever seen a lighthouse? At the top of a lighthouse is a big, bright light. When it's dark or foggy on the ocean, the keeper of the lighthouse shines that big light out over the water to show ships the way to reach the shore.

Jesus said He is the *Light of the World*. Light shows us what's really there and what is true. It shows us the right way to go. Just as the light from a lighthouse guides a ship to safety, Jesus guides us with His truth and light. And Jesus gives us His light to shine for others too!

Dear God, thank You for helping me shine Jesus' light to people who need to know Him. Please help me shine for Jesus! Amen.

LEARN MORE

Matthew 5:16 says, "Let your light shine before others, so that they may see your good works and give glory to your Father who is in heaven." Jesus wants everyone to know about Him because one day He will come again.

WHAT HAPPENED NEXT?

Saul became known as Paul. He made three different missionary trips to start new churches. He also wrote much of the New Testament. But the last book of the Bible was written by the disciple named John, who had the most amazing vision from God . . .

On a White Horse

He is Lord of lords and King of kings.
—Revelation 17:14

FROM MATTHEW 24–25; ACTS 1; REVELATION 19–22. Jesus' disciples had stared up into the sky and watched Jesus disappear into the clouds above the Mount of Olives as He went back to heaven. They had seen two angels dressed in white suddenly appear.

"Why are you looking into the sky?" the angels had asked. "One day, Jesus will come back to earth. He will come back the same way you just saw Him go."

Jesus had told them that once too. "Everyone on earth will see Me coming from heaven on the clouds, with great glory and power," He had said.

When will that be? the disciples wondered now. *And what will heaven be like?*

They had asked Jesus about it once, but Jesus had said, "Only God the Father knows when that day will come. So you must be ready every day, because you don't know what day it will be."

Many years later, while the disciple John lived on the island called Patmos, Jesus gave John a vision. In the vision, John saw what it will be like when Jesus comes back again.

First, John saw Jesus riding on a white horse. Jesus' eyes were bright like fire, and on His head, He wore many crowns. On His robe was written a name: "KING OF ALL KINGS AND LORD OF ALL LORDS." Behind Jesus, John saw the angel armies of heaven, all wearing robes of clean, white linen, and riding on white horses.

Then John saw a new heaven, a new earth, and a new heavenly city that shone like a beautiful jewel. The river from God's throne flowed through the city, and the Tree of Life grew on each side of the river. John heard a loud voice from the throne say, "Look, God is living with His people now! He will wipe every tear from their eyes, and there will be no more pain or sadness or death."

"I am the First and the Last, the Beginning and the End," Jesus said. "And I am coming soon!"

Amen! Come, Lord Jesus!

WHAT DOES IT MEAN?

Have you ever been to a fireworks show? The fireworks shoot up into the dark night sky—*Boom! Boom! Boom!* Then they explode with pops and sizzles into giant-sized, colorful designs. Sometimes the ground seems to shake. Sometimes the fireworks seem to dance to the music. When the grand finale comes, at the end of the show, so many fireworks light up the sky at the same time that it doesn't even feel like night at all.

That's how it will be when Jesus comes back. But the light will be from Jesus Himself, not from fireworks. Jesus is better than any other king who ever lived and better than any lord or governor or president. He is *King of kings*, and He rules forever. What a wonderful day it will be when Jesus comes back!

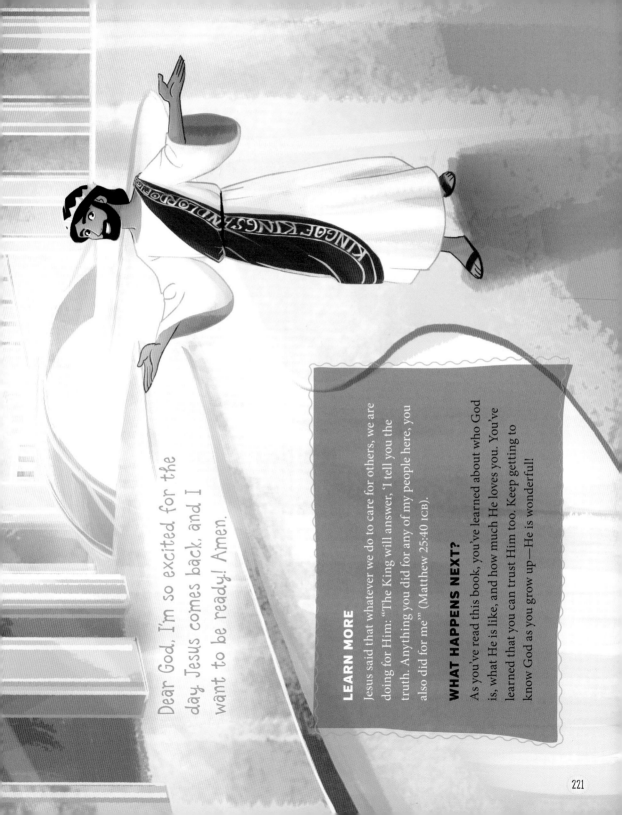

Dear God, I'm so excited for the day Jesus comes back, and I want to be ready! Amen.

LEARN MORE

Jesus said that whatever we do to care for others, we are doing for Him: "The King will answer, 'I tell you the truth. Anything you did for any of my people here, you also did for me'" (Matthew 25:40 ICB).

WHAT HAPPENS NEXT?

As you've read this book, you've learned about who God is, what He is like, and how much He loves you. You've learned that you can trust Him too. Keep getting to know God as you grow up—He is wonderful!

Learn More About the Names of God

If your family would like to learn more about God's names, here are some good books to help you get started.

FOR ADULTS

Daily Reflections on the Names of God by Ava Pennington (Revell)

Praying the Names of God and *Praying the Names of Jesus* by Ann Spangler (Zondervan)

FOR MIDDLE GRADE

God's Names by Sally Michael (P&R Publishing)

About the Author

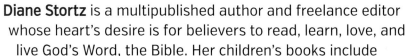

Diane Stortz is a multipublished author and freelance editor whose heart's desire is for believers to read, learn, love, and live God's Word, the Bible. Her children's books include *Words to Dream On: Bedtime Bible Stories and Prayers*; *Say & Pray Bible: First Words, Stories, and Prayers*; and *The Sweetest Story Bible: Sweet Thoughts and Sweet Words for Little Girls*. She also has written *A Woman's Guide to Reading the Bible in a Year* and coauthored *Parents of Missionaries: How to Thrive and Stay Connected When Your Children and Grandchildren Serve Cross-Culturally*.

Diane and her husband, Ed, a retired juvenile court probation officer, live in Cincinnati, Ohio. They have two married daughters and four young grandsons.

When she's not writing or editing, Diane enjoys walking, gardening, and planning her next trip to visit her grandkids.

Visit Diane at DianeStortz.com.

Diane Le Feyer is a French illustrator. Even as a child, she always knew that one day she would draw wonderful pictures for kids to enjoy! She also teaches students what she knows about illustration. Diane is very busy with her life as a teacher, artist, mother, Star Wars enthusiast, and bad cook. She has a darling daughter, a loving husband, and a pearlscale goldfish named Bubbles.